Optimal Currency Areas and the Euro, Volume I

Johannes Kabderian Dreyer ·
Peter Alfons Schmid

Optimal Currency Areas and the Euro, Volume I

Business Cycles Synchronization

palgrave
macmillan

Johannes Kabderian Dreyer
ISE
Roskilde University RUC
Roskilde, Denmark

Peter Alfons Schmid
FOM University of Applied Sciences
for Economics and Management
Munich, Germany

ISBN 978-3-030-46514-8 ISBN 978-3-030-46515-5 (eBook)
https://doi.org/10.1007/978-3-030-46515-5

This Palgrave Pivot imprint is published by the registered company Springer Nature Switzerland AG
The registered company address is: Gewerbestrasse 11, 6330 Cham, Switzerland

Preface

Even before its launch, economists questioned whether the Euro area (EA) has what it takes to become an optimal currency area (OCA). The onset of the sovereign debt crisis in 2010 confirmed challenges in its construction. But does the EA change over time, and which key drivers may be necessary in the future to strengthen it?

In this mini-series we use the theory of OCA and applied econometric techniques to provide a compact analysis of the EA, its evolution and future perspectives. In order to do so, we complement the literature by offering the reader a concise and broad view on the application to the EA of all three OCA criteria: Business Cycle Synchronization, Capital and Labor Mobility, and Risk Sharing Mechanisms. Our readers can thus use the pivot series as a handbook for EA economics.

We dedicate one pivot to each of the three main criteria and reflect upon how far the EA is from an OCA and whether this distance has been reduced during its existence endogenously. Identifying the key drivers for a better fulfillment of the OCA criteria allows us to suggest policies that could serve this purpose.

The main audience for this series is formed by scholars and advanced students in the fields of macroeconomics, econometrics, and management. They can use our contribution as reference for their own research. Advanced graduate students could also use the pivot series in class to learn static and dynamic econometric methodologies based on our empirical work. Although not necessarily restricted to these, examples for potential target courses are Public Economics, European Economics,

Applied Econometrics, and Quantitative Methods in Business Studies and Economics. Finally, policymakers get an overview of the main arguments in the OCA discussion that contributes to their work.

Roskilde, Denmark Johannes Kabderian Dreyer
Munich, Germany Peter Alfons Schmid

Acknowledgments We would like to thank fellow scholars who contributed with their knowledge and rigor to this book: two anonymous referees, Prof. Dr. Kristian Sund and Ass. Prof. Dr. Marcelo Klötzle who helped to review and discuss content and materials. Lastly, special thanks to Eva Bisgaard Pedersen who carefully proofread the manuscript.

Contents

About the Authors

Johannes Kabderian Dreyer earned his bachelor's degree in Economics and completed his master's in Finance at the Pontifical Catholic University of Rio de Janeiro. Afterwards, he defended his doctorate in Financial Economics at the Catholic University of Eichstätt-Ingolstadt. Today, he is Associate Professor of Financial Economics at Roskilde University.

Peter Alfons Schmid earned his diploma degree and doctorate at the Catholic University of Eichstätt-Ingolstadt. He was teaching and research assistant, worked as a professional at global and regional accounting firms, and developed a tech start-up. Today, he is Professor of Business Administration at the FOM University of Applied Sciences.

List of Figures

Chapter 2

Chapter 3

Chapter 4

Appendix 2: An Introduction to Multiple Regressions

List of Tables

Chapter 4

Appendix 2: An Introduction to Multiple Regressions

CHAPTER 1

Introduction

Abstract By shortly discussing the three criteria of Optimal Currency Areas proposed by Mundell in 1961 and its application to the Euro area (EA), this first chapter presents our pivot series. Moreover, it introduces the content of this first pivot "Business Cycles Synchronization," discussing its importance for currency unions and more specifically for the EA. The chapter further offers brief comments on the results of the analysis of business cycle synchronization that was conducted throughout the pivot.

Keywords Euro · Optimal currency areas · Synchronization of business cycles · Factor mobility · Risk sharing mechanism · Presentation of analysis

The Euro is the latest and deepest step of economic integration of 19 member countries in the European Union (short: EU). These member countries constitute the Euro area (short: EA) through the introduction of a single currency. It functions as a system of irreversible fixed exchange rates as national currencies were given up entirely.

Back in 1992, member states of the then called European Communities laid the fundaments for the EA as they agreed upon the creation of the European System of Central Banks (short: ESCB) and the European Central Bank (short: ECB). A common European currency that would be later called Euro was set to replace national currencies (Kenen 1995, 1). All EU

J. Kabderian Dreyer and P. A. Schmid,
Optimal Currency Areas and the Euro, Volume I,
https://doi.org/10.1007/978-3-030-46515-5_1

member countries[1] obliged themselves to eventually join the Euro (European Commission 2019). Eleven EU countries started to share a common currency in 1999 and eight more joined the following years. As of today, there have been no exits from this single currency club, although such were discussed politically and in academia for some countries during Europe's sovereign debt crisis (see *inter alia* Auerback 2010; Crum 2013; Overbeek 2012).

The expectation of economic benefits as a result of sharing a common currency is not new. Already back in the nineteenth century John Stuart Mill, philosopher and economist and one of the most prominent thinkers of classical liberalism stated: "*So much of barbarism, however, still remains in the transactions of most civilised nations, that almost all independent countries choose to assert their nationality by having, to their inconvenience and that of their neighbours, a peculiar currency of their own*" (Mill 2004, 572).

In line with Mill, EA members should expect a growth bonus. At least, this is in the Euro's promise: economically, a common currency shared by different regions or countries increases integration.[2] Entrepreneurs benefit from decreased uncertainty with respect to future prices for their foreign sales, procurement and from larger integrated markets that foster economies of scale. Consumers benefit from increased product varieties that better meet their needs and can enjoy greater utility in case of love-for-variety preferences. Competition enhances efficiency and promotes technological progress, in other words higher total factor productivity. However, so far this growth bonus has not materialized empirically (inter alia Dreyer and Schmid 2017).

Per definition, monetary policy is uniform for all EA member countries. Its primary goal of keeping inflation close to but below two percent has been reached since the Euro's start in 1999. Recently, inflation rates have been well below the two percent limit but not negative. This, however, is no exception as other industrialized countries and, especially, EU members without the Euro have had very low inflation rates as well. Consequently, the Euro has not failed *prima vista*. Nevertheless, there have been many skeptics at both political and academic levels that have criticized the decision to introduce the Euro.

[1] Denmark has an opt-out and has no obligation to join, the same was valid for the UK. Other countries like Sweden can postpose joining by not participating in the so-called exchange rate mechanism II which is a formal prerequisite for future members.

[2] For a chronological overview of the European Integration, see Appendix 1.

Some scholars have been concerned about the viability of the Euro as a common currency area because of increased stabilization costs that might outweigh the benefits of lower transaction costs. As early as 1990, Eichengreen (1990) stated that the EU was not prepared for a common currency as, in comparison to the United States, the EU lacked a system of fiscal federalism and showed only limited labor mobility. Friedman (1997) even predicted the risk of political tensions in the EU as flexible exchange rates cannot serve their role of automatic stabilizers in case of asymmetric economic shocks to single member countries. In his words: "*I believe that adoption of the Euro would have the opposite effect. It would exacerbate political tensions by converting divergent shocks that could have been readily accommodated by exchange rate changes into divisive political issues*" (Friedman 1997). Along the same lines, Feldstein (1997) called the Euro an economic liability for its members, arguing that "*a single currency would cause at most small trade and investment gains but would raise average cyclical unemployment and would probably raise inflation, perpetuate structural unemployment, and increase the risk of protectionism*" (Feldstein 1997, Abstract).

However, other scholars have been more positive about the EA project without neglecting the necessary further work to make a single currency area work. Obstfeld and Peri (1998) wrote before the Euro's start: "*EMU is about to be born, however, only because Europe has shown the creativity and determination to meet (..) challenges in the past. The same qualities will be needed in abundance to make EMU work*" (Obstfeld and Peri 1998, 49).

So how well is the single currency faring today, more than twenty years after its birth?

1 Introduction to the Pivot Series

In this series of three pivots we set out to discuss the success of the EA more than two decades following its launch. We look at the work done so far and discuss what is still needed for the EA to be considered successful. We will build our investigation around the theory of optimal currency areas (short: OCA), analyzing the EA against the three OCA criteria that according to the theory need to be present for a currency area to be successful: (1) synchronization of business cycles, (2) factor mobility, and (3) risk sharing mechanism. We dedicate a pivot to each of the three criteria. We cover the basic ideas of each criterion and measure their degree of existence in the EA empirically. We use linear regressions to answer the following questions:

- Which variables determine business cycle synchronization and what can be learned from an EA perspective? (pivot 1)
- Did labor and capital mobility dampen asymmetric shocks among regions during the short history of the Euro? (pivot 2)
- Did the EA stability mechanism work as expected from a risk sharing mechanism such as a fiscal federalism system? (pivot 3)

Answers to these questions allow us to indicate the distance of the EA from an OCA and whether this distance has become shorter during the Euro's existence endogenously. Moreover, we will show how these criteria can be met in a better way and, thus, derive policy recommendations that can serve this purpose.

1.1 Criteria of Optimum Currency Areas

The OCA criteria were developed by Mundell (1961), Kenen (1969) and McKinnon (1963). Mundell, himself a Canadian, was concerned by the differences between Canadian provinces that might not be well-prepared to share a common currency. The same could be said for the United States which provoked Mundell's hypothesis that the borderline for the US and Canadian Dollar shall not separate the North from the South but the East from the West, grouping Western Canadian provinces and US states as well as their Eastern cousins together in two currency areas (Mundell 1961, 660).

For Mundell, a common currency is the final stage of economic integration between at least two regions, which can be separate countries or different regions within the same country. The crucial question for every possible currency union is whether the advantages outweigh its negative implications. For this purpose, the three OCA criteria can be used to evaluate the suitability of potential members.

In the following, we shortly introduce each of the three OCA criteria further.

1.2 Synchronization of Business Cycles Across Regions (Topic of Pivot 1)

For a successful common currency area, it is pivotal that the macroeconomic dynamics of the different regions inside the area are similar. Synchronized business cycles yield comparable price dynamics. This makes it easier for a central monetary authority to achieve its primary aim; inflation control: it can apply a unique monetary policy across all regions, with a view to accelerate inflation in case of deflationary pressure and contain inflation in case of rates above the inflation target. Moreover, it becomes easier to dampen both booms and recessions along the business cycle; the important secondary goal of macroeconomic stabilization.

The central monetary authority could follow an expansionary approach during recessions and a contractionary one during booms. According to the Taylor rule, the monetary authority should orientate its nominal interest rates toward the gap between inflationary expectations and the inflation target as well as toward the output gap (De Grauwe 2018, 192). This endeavor becomes a mission impossible in case of varying gaps across different regions of a currency union. A good example is the EA in the early 2000s with the burst of the dot.com bubble hitting Germany and the core harder than the periphery. Fiscal policy responses were limited by the Stability and Growth Pact, and looser (expansionary) monetary policy was implemented in the EA (Koo 2012). As a result, a credit boom in medium- or low-tech activities in the EA's periphery was financed by capital flows from the core (Storm and Naastepad 2015). The core, on the contrary, did not benefit much from the loose monetary policy (Koo 2012). The reverse was postulated in the aftermath of the financial crisis and during the sovereign debt crisis in the early 2010s. The expansionary monetary policy of the European Central Bank (short: ECB) fueled an export boom in Germany but increased the EA's underlying problem, the core's very large current account surpluses (Patelis 2015).

In case synchronized business cycles are present, the other two OCA criteria become less important, as a central monetary authority such as the European Central Bank can adjust symmetric shocks via a common monetary policy. In case of full synchronization, the same monetary policy is suitable and stabilization costs are, thus, not increased as a result of irreversible, fixed exchange rates. Consequently, flexible exchange rates are not needed as an automatic stabilizer.

In the case of disentangled business cycles, however, asymmetric shocks make the two other OCA criteria important for the well-functioning of currency unions.

1.3 Capital and Labor Mobility Across Regions (Topic of Pivot 2)

Factor mobility across regions ensure capital and labor flows that dampen the impact of asymmetric shocks. Imagine that only a single region is hit by a recession which increases unemployment due to lower aggregate demand resulting in lower production and income. Migration from the affected region to others where labor is needed, and thus where marginal returns to labor are higher, lowers the socio-economic problem. This way, an excess of labor supply is automatically compensated with migration avoiding the need of customized monetary policies. Thus, this reaction of workers has a buffering effect.

Due to language and cultural barriers and relatively high rigidity, labor mobility naturally plays a smaller role in the EU than in the United States (Beyer and Smets 2015). Arpaia et al. (2016) summarized the role of labor mobility in the EU with the following words: "*Cross-country mobility flows in the EU are still much lower than those recorded in other highly integrated economic areas, notably the USA, and well below mobility within countries. The population of migrants from within the EU is also generally much lower than the population of migrants from outside the EU. Nevertheless, an upward trend in mobility is visible in the EU, not only as a result of the enlargement.*"

Capital mobility is seen as another adjustment mechanism in the event of asymmetric shocks in currency unions (Ingram 1959). When capital mobility is perfect, the natural forces of supply and demand should allocate resources and investments according to where they carry the largest fruits and are needed. With capital mobility asymmetric shocks on domestic savings do not matter for domestic investment. In such cases, capital inflow from foreign savings would counterbalance the lack of domestic ones. As the Euro eliminated exchange rate volatility, current account policies were expected to lose their importance, and tax competition should have narrowed tax differentials so that capital mobility was expected to increase with the introduction of the Euro (Stirböck and Heinemann 1999, 20).

Even before the common currency, the European Union experienced deeper financial integration through the abolition of capital controls and the harmonization of financial regulations. In addition, the Euro removed the currency risk for member countries. As a result, obstacles to capital mobility decreased considerably within the EA, the home bias decreased and financial trade increased (Lane 2009; Lane and Milesi-Ferretti 2008). But despite the spectacular boom of capital flows in the early years of the Euro, capital mobility proved to act in a destabilizing way during the financial crisis. The EA experienced a boom-bust cycle that was larger than similar cycles observed in the broader European region and in the global set of advanced economies.

1.4 *Risk Sharing Mechanism Between Regions (Topic of Pivot 3)*

In case of asynchronous business cycles and imperfect factor mobility, risk sharing via fiscal transfers is a possible means for keeping stabilization costs low in a single currency area. Such a risk sharing system incorporates a mechanism that transfers resources to those regions that are affected asymmetrically. Within a single region or country common systems of social security and centralized spending usually serve the role of risk sharing. When a region is hit, unemployment benefits that are financed commonly increase in this region. The central government can, in addition, foster economic growth in single regions by allocating its resources there, e.g., by the installment of military facilities or administrative governmental units.

EA member countries historically relied on systems of fiscal federalism, contrary to the United States where labor mobility plays a much more important role for adjustment to asymmetric shocks (Obstfeld and Peri 1998). Consequently, it was feared that "*the EU will face strong pressures to expand its centralized fiscal functions in the direction of inter-country stabilization transfers. Given the generally high persistence of macroeconomic shocks in Europe, especially shocks at the national level, stabilization payments are likely to play a substantial ex post redistributive role as well*" (Obstfeld and Peri 1998, 44). In line with this argument, Dreyer and Schmid (2015) simulate the costs of such a system of fiscal federalism for each EA member.

The argument of a pure insurance scheme within the EA looks alluring, but potentially feeds moral hazard and brings political destabilization (Obstfeld and Peri 1998). Politically this would imply transferring tax income from one country to another. With more countries, there are usually more obstacles for the implementation of fiscal transfers. Nevertheless, the EA developed the European Stability Mechanism (ESM) giving financial assistance to member countries with severe financing problems as a reaction to the European sovereign debt crisis (Oręziak 2018). Other evolvements like a European monetary fund or uniform insurances schemes are being discussed at the time of writing (Berger et al. 2019). One could argue that ESM loans differ from fiscal transfers because they need to be redeemed. However, we can claim that these loans work in the EA similarly to fiscal transfers, since they have very long maturities and are guaranteed not only by the recipient country but by all EA members.[3] Thus, we can compare ESM loans in the EA to stabilization transfers.

1.5 Using the OCA Criteria to Evaluate the Entrance of New Members

The argument for regions sharing a common currency becomes smaller, *ceteris paribus*, the further a currency union is from fulfilling the three criteria. The costs of counteraction of asymmetric shocks increase, and it becomes costlier for a region or a country to become a member. The lack of power to counteract asymmetric shocks can lead to significant losses in the real economy. Floating exchange rates, to the contrast, can become more appropriate since they would work as an automatic adjustment mechanism for the real economy. Thus, it is a natural straightforward question to ask to which extent do EA members as a group form an OCA. In case of shortcomings one might ask whether the currency union itself produced more accordance with the OCA criteria. These questions will be answered in the pivot series at hand.

2 More About Business Cycles Synchronization and the Euro

This first volume is dedicated to study synchronization in business cycles in the EA, the first criterion set by Mundell to qualify regions into OCAs.

2.1 Synchronized Business Cycles and Common Monetary Policy

During the last decades, business cycles have become increasingly synchronized globally (De Grauwe and Ji 2017). This development has presumably originated from increased financial integration for country-specific shocks (Cesa-Bianchi et al. 2016) and the dissemination of common global waves of optimism and pessimism (De Grauwe and Ji 2017). People share expectations for the future economic

[3] Data on the different rates and maturities of loans granted to EA member countries can be found at: https://www.esm.europa.eu/financial-assistance. Loan repayments, for example, are scheduled until 2060 for programs that ended in 2018. Average maturities vary from 12.5 (i.e., Spain) to 32.35 (i.e., Greece) years.

development and adapt their decisions accordingly. For instance, a global wave of pessimism facilitates a worldwide economic downturn with regular downward adjustments of expected short-term growth rates, both globally and regionally. Such global self-fulfilling prophecies produce further synchronization.

The advent of more synchronization favors the well-functioning of currency unions even though business cycles are not perfect positively correlated and their intensities vary immensely. Potential recessions are usually counteracted with lower nominal central bank interest rates and quantitative easing, with the hope that lower real interest rates will stimulate demand. In the light of continuously low inflation rates and the economic downturn in the EA, the ECB acted accordingly in the autumn of 2019 by further lowering the rate on the deposit facility to −0.50% and by restarting net asset purchases.[4]

Conversely, in case of economic boom, higher interest rates and a contraction of the rate of money growth work against an overheating of the economy. Thus, the general type of monetary policy is the same for all members in a currency union and tends to work well in case their business cycles are synchronized.

If deeper economic integration increases synchronization, one could argue that the EA better meets the first OCA criterium simply by its existence (the "endogeneity argument"). There is, however, no common view whether the Euro itself favors or disfavors synchronization. Although the "endogeneity view" is popular, it is heavily disputed. In Chapter 2 we review relevant literature on the need of business cycle synchronization, starting with the canonical AS–AD model. We further elaborate on the transmission channels for (dis)synchronization. It is possible, for example, that economic integration yields specialization (e.g., commodity industry in Canada's Western provinces and manufacturing industry in its Eastern parts). We present a discussion of a set of variables that may have effects on business cycle synchronization, among other economic specialization and trade variables. Thereby, we lay the ground for the empirical investigation of Chapter 3.

[4]Although the entire EA was in a downturn, the decision in the ECB's Governing Council was, however, not unanimous and there was much disaffirmation from economists from different parts of the EA, not only—as suspected—from Germany and Northern members. This is due to general discomfort with the new normal of very low interest rates and valid concerns about its long-term consequences.

In Chapter 3 we run a descriptive analysis on the cycle components of GDPs of different countries to measure their level of synchronization, where higher correlations indicate higher synchronization. In order to do so, we use the Baxter–King bandpass filter to extract the GDP's cyclical component.

The descriptive analysis of correlation coefficients of the cyclical components of the GDP of the different pairs of countries offers two important key learnings:

- Business cycles among EA member countries are more correlated than among US states. Although, the United States is regarded as an established currency union, there is less synchronization on the Western shore of the Atlantic in comparison to the Eastern shore.
- There has been a global trend toward more synchronized business cycles globally in the last decades. During and after the sovereign debt crisis in the EA, there was, however, less synchronization.

In the second part of Chapter 3 we regress the bilateral correlation coefficients on a set of distance variables as defined in Chapter 2. These variables include economic and trade specialization, differentials of real interest rates, government deficits and effective exchange rates, exchange rate volatility, a set of trade variables, i.e., relative bilateral trade volumes and general trade openness, and financial integration measured by foreign assets and liabilities. Moreover, geographical distance and population gravity are considered. The key findings are:

- The estimates of most simple regressions have the expected signs and most of them are statistically significant.
- Based on the Akaike information criterion we select different multiple regression models where we are generally able to observe the same expected signs for our estimates.
- Economic specialization generally was not significant. This changes when we account for financial integration. In this case, the variable has a negative relation with synchronization. On the other hand, trade specialization has a negative relation with specialization. The same is valid to interest rate and deficit differentials.
- All three variables for trade intensity have generally a positive relationship with correlations. However, when capital stocks are considered this is not any longer true.

- Volatility of exchange rates and differences in real effective exchange rates have a negative relation with correlations.
- Before and after the European debt crisis the level of synchronization is lower. During the crisis business cycles are more synchronized due to the common shock.
- Membership in the EA has a positive effect on synchronization. Only during the run-up to the financial crisis there is less synchronization for EA member countries.
- Capital stocks have a positive relationship with correlations. Even though in some of the models this variable is not significant to determine correlations, this is not the same for EA countries. In their case, bilateral positions in capital stocks have a positive relation to synchronization that is weakly significant.

Based thereon, we draw conclusions in Chapter 4 and discuss variables that should be of special interest for policymakers if one aims to facilitate higher business cycle synchronization across EA member countries.

References

Arpaia, A., Kiss, A., Palvolgyi, B., & Turrini, A. (2016). Labour Mobility and Labour Market Adjustment in the EU. *IZA Journal of Migration, 5,* 21.

Auerback, M. (2010). A "United States of Europe" or Full Exit from the Euro? *International Journal of Political Economy, 39*(4), 87–102.

Berger, H., Dell'Ariccia, G., & Obstfeld, M. (2019). Revisiting the Economic Case for Fiscal Union in the Euro Area. *IMF Economic Review, 67,* 657–683.

Beyer, R. C. M., & Smets, F. (2015). Labour Market Adjustments and Migration in Europe and the United States: How Different? *Economic Policy, 30*(84), 643–682.

Cesa-Bianchi, A., Imbs, J., & Saleheen, J. (2016). *Finance and Synchronization* (CEPR Discussion Paper, 11037).

Crum, B. (2013). Saving the Euro at the Cost of Democracy? *Journal of Common Market Studies, 51*(4), 614–630.

De Grauwe, P. (2018). *Economics of Monetary Union* (12th ed.). Oxford: Oxford University Press.

De Grauwe, P., & Ji, Y. (2017). The International Synchronisation of Business Cycles: The Role of Animal Spirits. *Open Economic Review, 28,* 383–412.

Dreyer, J. K., & Schmid, P. A. (2015). Fiscal Federalism in Monetary Unions: Hypothetical Fiscal Transfers Within the Euro-Zone. *International Review of Applied Economics, 29*(4), 506–532.

Dreyer, J. K., & Schmid, P. A. (2017). Growth Effects of EU and EZ Memberships: Empirical Findings from the First 15 Years of the Euro. *Economic Modelling, 67*, 45–54.

Eichengreen, B. (1990). One Money for Europe? *Lessons from the US Currency Union, Economic Policy, 5*(10), 117–187.

Feldstein, M. (1997). The Political Economy of the European Economic and Monetary Union: Political Sources of an Economic Liability. *Journal of Economic Perspectives, 11*(4), 23–42.

Ingram, J. (1959). State and Regional Payments Mechanisms. *Quarterly Journal of Economics, 73*(4), 619–632.

Kenen, P. (1969). The Theory of Optimum Currency Areas: An Eclectic View. In R. Mundell & A. Swoboda (Eds.), *Monetary Problems of the International Economy*. Chicago: University of Chicago Press.

Kenen, P. (1995). *Economic and Monetary Union in Europe*. Cambridge: Cambridge University Press.

Koo, R. (2012, October 14). *Balance Sheet Recession as the Other Half of Macroeconomics*. Nomura Research Institute.

Lane, P. R. (2009). EMU and Financial Integration. In B. Mackowiak, F. Mongelli, G. Noblet, & F. Smets (Eds.), *The Euro at Ten—Lessons and Challenges* (pp. 82–115). Frankfurt am Main: European Central Bank.

Lane, P. R., & Milesi-Ferretti, G. M. (2008). The Drivers of Financial Globalization. *American Economic Review (Papers & Proceedings), 98*(2), 327–332.

McKinnon, R. (1963). Optimum Currency Areas. *American Economic Review, 53*(4), 717–725.

Mill, J. S. (2004). *Principles of Political Economy*. London: Prometheus Books and Pennsylvania State University.

Mundell, R. (1961). A Theory of Optimum Currency Areas. *The American Economic Review, 51*(4), 657–665.

Obstfeld, M., & Peri, G. (1998). Regional Nonadjustment and Fiscal Policy. *Economic Policy, 26*, 205–259.

Oręziak, L. (2018). Fiscal Federalism and a Separate Budget for the Euro Area. *International Journal of Management and Economics, 54*(2), 85–98.

Overbeek, H. (2012). Sovereign Debt Crisis in Euroland: Root Causes and Implications for European Integration. *The International Spectator, 47*(1), 30–48.

Patelis, A. (2015). The Elephant in the Euro Room. In D. D. Thomakos, P. Monokroussos, & K. I. Nikolopoulos (Eds.), *A Financial Crisis Manual: Palgrave Macmillan Studies in Banking and Financial Institutions*. London: Palgrave Macmillan.

Stirböck, C., and Heinemann, F. (1999). *Capital Mobility Within EMU* (ZEW Discussion Papers, No. 99-19).

Storm, S., & Naastepad, C. W. M. (2015). NAIRU Economics and the Eurozone Crisis. *International Review of Applied Economics, 29*(6), 843–877.

Internet Sources

European Commission. (2019). *Who Can Join and When?* Available at: https://ec.europa.eu/info/business-economy-euro/euro-area/enlargement-euro-area/who-can-join-and-when_en. Accessed November 26, 2019.

Friedman, M. (1997). *The Euro: Monetary Unity to Political Disunity*. Available at: https://www.project-syndicate.org/commentary/the-euro–monetary-unity-to-political-disunity. Accessed November 26, 2019.

CHAPTER 2

Literature and Theory

Abstract This chapter performs an in-depth analysis of the literature on Business Cycles Synchronization showing its importance to currency unions, where members are not able to conduct monetary policies on their own. Moreover, it presents economic variables that are commonly used by the literature to study the synchronization of business cycles. Finally, the chapter presents conflicting theories on the capacity of the EA to evolve toward more synchronization over time.

Keywords Synchronization variables · AS–AD model · Fixed and flexible exchange rates · Stabilization · Monetary and fiscal policies · Financial twist · Endogeneity in business cycles

Stabilization mechanisms through traditional fiscal and monetary policies are hard to implement in currency unions whose different regions are not affected in the same manner by economic shocks, making stabilization more complicated and costlier. Despite the promises of deeper economic integration "***virtually any US state can attest, an integrated continental market does not solve all local problems, and can even make some of them worse***" (Krugman 1993, 260).

In closed economies, traditional economic measures, such as Keynesian policies to counter adverse economic shocks, may be the right medicine in the event of demand shocks. In open economies, however,

J. Kabderian Dreyer and P. A. Schmid,
Optimal Currency Areas and the Euro, Volume I,
https://doi.org/10.1007/978-3-030-46515-5_2

especially in the presence of capital mobility—and thus a uniform global interest rate—the transmission mechanism of such policies is disturbed (Mundell 1963).

For example, fixed exchange rates make monetary policy ineffective, as an increasing money supply with downward pressure on interest rates produces a capital outflow that must be countered with the sale of foreign reserves. This is necessary in order to keep the exchange rate constant (Mundell 1963). Imagine a central bank that reduces its nominal rates or buys assets in exchange for liquidity: both measures aim at a reduction of domestic real interest rates. With capital mobility, investors will search for higher returns in foreign capital markets and thus transfer liquidity abroad. Thereby, demand for foreign currencies is created and, *ceteris paribus*, will depreciate the domestic currency. To keep the exchange rate constant the central bank must react and sell its foreign reserves in exchange for domestic currency.

In an open economy without currency union, the exchange rate can serve the role as an automatic stabilizer, in case floating exchange rates are allowed. Currency unions, however, can be seen as a system of fixed and irreversible exchange rates. Real devaluation, thus, only materializes in the medium run by nominal price adjustments. In the meantime, price rigidities, especially on labor markets, yield unemployment and lower participation rates if the unemployed do not migrate to greener pastures.

In the following we will highlight the complications of stabilization policies in common currency areas using the well-known model framework of aggregate supply and demand (the AS–AD model). We will show why synchronized business cycles are a prerequisite for uniform policies and, second, elaborate which and how factors impact business cycle synchronization.

1 The AS–AD Model

The canonical aggregate supply–aggregate demand (short: AS–AD) textbook model distinguishes demand and supply shocks. Demand shocks have only temporary effects on output, while supply shocks have permanent ones. Both types of shocks, though, have permanent effects on prices. Aggregate demand and aggregate supply are drawn in a price–output plane as in Fig. 1.

The AD curve has a negative slope as a higher amount of real money boosts aggregate demand. The economic rationale is as follows: falling

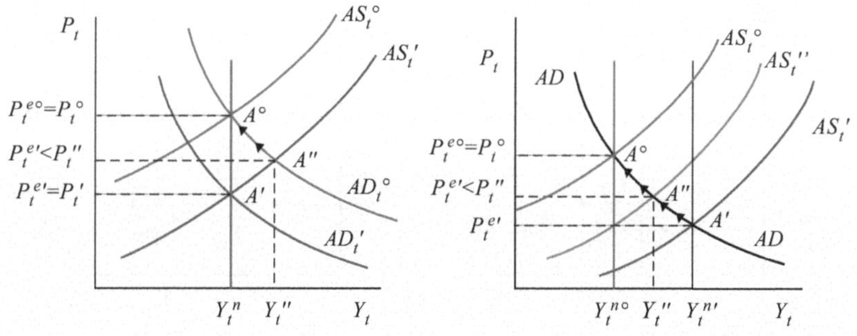

Fig. 1 AS–AD model with positive demand shock (l.h.s.) and negative supply shock (r.h.s.) (*Source* Authors)

prices increase the real money supply. An equilibrium on money markets requires interest rates to fall. Lower interest rates in turn increase current consumption that becomes cheaper in comparison to future consumption. *Ceteris paribus*, investment increases as the current values of investment projects increase. The AS curve has a positive slope in the short run because real wages decrease with a higher price level, in case of sticky nominal wages. Lower real wages increase employment and the economy's output. In the long run, however, the AS curve is vertical, as nominal wages adjust to higher prices. The long-run natural output level is solely determined by the potential of economic production given by the available quantities and qualities of production factors.

A positive demand shock (l.h.s. of Fig. 1) shifts the AD curve to the right, from AD'_t to AD°_t, with the short-run equilibrium moving from A' to A''. In the short run prices increase to P''_t, output to Y''_t and real wages fall. In the medium run the AS curve moves upwards. This pushes prices up to P°_t yielding the new equilibrium A° with higher prices and the same natural output Y^n_t.

Why? In the short-run price expectation $P^{e'}_t$ are equal to the price level in the former short-run equilibrium A'. The actual price level in the new short-run equilibrium A'' is higher. The gap between actual prices and price expectations cause workers to adjust their nominal wage demands. Because of the higher nominal price levels producers are not reluctant to grant such hikes. Consequently, nominal wages will increase in the medium run due to requests for higher wages to compensate for the unexpected higher level of prices. Wages begin to raise and push back

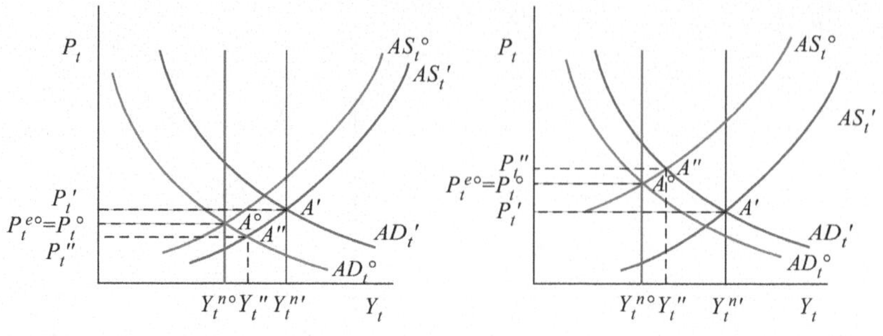

Fig. 2 AS–AD model with negative demand shock with supply response (left) and negative supply shock with demand response (right) (*Source* Authors)

the AS curve yielding the long-run vertical AS curve (the vertical line). In the long-run equilibrium A° price expectations and the price level concur, again. The output effect of a demand shock, thus, is only temporary.

A negative supply shock, on the contrary, has permanent price and output responses. The AS curve is shifted upwards from AS_t' to AS_t'' (r.h.s. of Fig. 1). Every output level is only feasible at higher prices. The lower output Y_t'' at the price level P_t'' does not constitute a long-run equilibrium as price expectations and prices fall apart. The adjustment shifts the AS curve further upwards to AS_t° until the price level and price expectations meet in the equilibrium with decreased output $Y_t^{n\circ}$ and increased price level P_t°. In the long run the aggregate supply curve again rotates to be vertical (left vertical line).

So far, we assumed shifts of aggregate demand and aggregate supply to be independent from each other. But there might be linkages which lead to hysteresis (Blanchard et al. 2015). There are different possibilities for how demand and supply shocks are interlinked. The effect of short-run unemployment due to a negative shock in demand is of high importance. Unemployment degrades the labor force yielding a lower future output potential. The same happens in case firms cut back investments as a response to temporary output reductions, which makes them permanent. The l.h.s. of Fig. 2 shows such a negative demand shock (from AD_t' to AD_t°) twisted with a decline in the output potential. The latter shifts aggregate supply upwards instead of downwards as expected in the canonical model. Thus, output does not return to its former natural level $Y_1^{n'}$ but to its new natural level Y_2^{no} (given by the left vertical line). The price level decreases to P_t°.

Moreover, a negative aggregate supply shock might shift aggregate demand in anticipation of lower income streams in the future, a scenario shown on the r.h.s. of Fig. 2. Consumers and investors expect output levels and as a result income streams for labor and capital to be lower in the future. According to the permanent income hypothesis, behavior is adjusted, with consumers lowering consumption levels and investors cutting back current investment, as higher investment levels would lead to lower marginal fruits of capital stocks. Consequently, output reduces to the new natural level Y_t^{no} (given by the left vertical line) but prices do not increase as much as in the case of no demand response. Lower aggregate demand dampens the effect on the price level.

1.1 Stabilization in the AS–AD Model

For negative demand shocks the textbook usually recommends a Keynesian approach with expansionary fiscal or monetary policy. This is assumed to shift back the AD curve, cushioning the output reduction. In addition, in an open economy with flexible exchange rates, devaluation of the domestic currency serves the role as an automatic stabilizer. When nominal prices do not adjust in the short run, a lower nominal exchange rate makes domestic goods and services relatively cheaper and, thus, cushions the demand shock. Monetary expansion, for example, might lower interest rates, which decreases the outside value of the domestic currency and stimulates net exports to the rest of the world.

This stabilization mechanism is damaged in currency unions whose different regions are not affected in the same manner by economic shocks, making stabilization more complicated and costlier. Differences are usually ascribed to idiosyncratic shocks that only affect one region, but can also be the result of common shocks. The financial crisis, for example, was a common shock to all industrialized countries but had different effects in the EA member countries. Whereas Greece, Portugal, Spain, Ireland, and Italy suffered from a lasting loss of confidence and capital outflows, the downturn in Germany, Austria, the Netherlands, and other countries was sharp but only of very short duration.

To understand the argument of higher stabilization costs, we consider two regions A and B that are initially in equilibrium with full

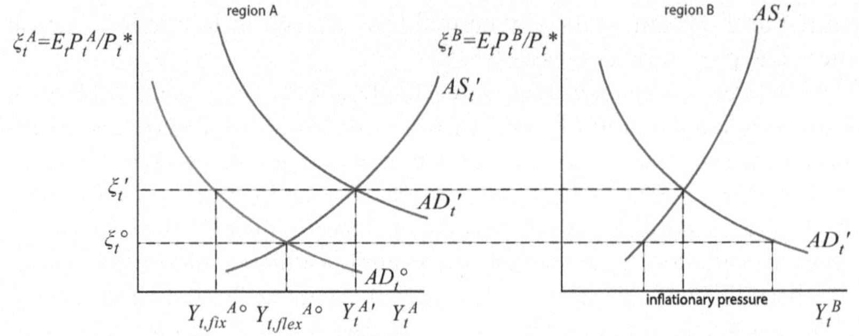

Fig. 3 Demand shock in region A with output gap in region A or inflationary pressure in region B (*Source* Authors)

employment. Region A shall be affected by a negative demand shock shifting its aggregate demand curve from $AD_t^{'}$ to AD_t° (see l.h.s. of Fig. 3). Please note that the ordinate labels the real exchange rate $\xi_t = E_t P_t / P_t^*$ where E_t is the nominal exchange rate in quantity notation and P_t^* the foreign price level. The lower demand for region *A's* goods and services will reduce region *A's* currency value immediately. The decreasing nominal exchange rate leads to real devaluation, i.e., a decline of the real exchange rate from $\xi_t^{'}$ to ξ_t°, limiting the short-run output contraction to $Y_t^{A'} - Y_{t,flex}^{A\circ}$ instead of $Y_t^{A'} - Y_{t,fix}^{A\circ}$, as displayed on the l.h.s. of Fig. 3. In addition, region A's central bank might follow the Keynesian approach and expand the monetary base to shift region *A's* aggregate demand curve back to the right. A regime of flexible exchange rates, thus, serves macroeconomic stabilization in the presence of nominal price and wage stickiness as the initial output contraction is smaller than in the case of fixed exchange rates.

If region *A*, however, forms a currency union with an unaffected region *B*, there is no flexible exchange rate. As a result, the output contraction would be much higher in region *A*, namely $Y_t^{A'} - Y_{t,fix}^{A\circ}$, in comparison to $Y_t^{A'} - Y_{t,flex}^{A\circ}$ in the case of flexible exchange rates. To close this gap expansionary monetary or fiscal efforts are necessary. Moreover, the risk of subsequent output shocks due to devaluation of the labor force and lower investment increases. In region B, to the contrary, the desired monetary expansion (from the perspective of region A) would generate inflationary pressure (see r.h.s. of Fig. 3).

Worse, in case of a pure asymmetric shock, where a positive shock in one region is entirely offset by a negative shock in the other region, the central monetary authority cannot see the need for demand stabilization. Aggregate demand still ensures the natural level of output (De Grauwe 2018, 190).

In a nutshell, there is no one-fits-all monetary policy in the case of asymmetric business cycles. Mundell (1961) described this dilemma the following way: "*[...] a currency area of either type cannot prevent both unemployment and inflation among its members. The fault line lies not with the type of currency area, but with the domain of the currency area*" (Mundell 1961, 659).

> **Nota bene**: Larger asymmetry in the impact of economic shocks increases the costs of a currency union ceteris paribus as stabilization policies are costlier or close to impossible due to a uniform monetary policy. This argument is especially virulent in case currency unions make asymmetrical disturbances likelier.

The cost argument of currency unions is strengthened by the limitation of possibilities of fiscal policy at the regional level. Although there should be a primacy for fiscal policy in currency unions, regions tend to follow procyclical fiscal policies like in the United States (Krugman 1993). In case of symmetric shocks, overall monetary policy in the currency union can accomplish stabilization. On the other hand, in case of asymmetric shocks, permanent adjustments (Blanchard and Katz 1992) on the regional level cannot, in practice, be remedied by regional fiscal policy. In the United States most states have constitutional provisions for balanced budgets and in the EA the European Fiscal Compact limits the room for fiscal policy at the national level beyond the former Stability and Growth Pact. This stricter version of the Stability and Growth Pact was agreed upon by all 19 EA members and by most other EU countries in 2012.[1]

A related problem is the difference in inflation rates across the regions of a currency union. It is well-known that the dynamics of the real exchange rate follow those of the nominal exchange rate and also the differences in inflation rates. In case of fixed or irreversible nominal exchange rates like in currency unions, the real exchange rate just

[1]The Czech Republic and Croatia who was not an EU member back in 2012 did not sign up.

moves according to the difference of inflation rates. In case of lower inflation in other regions there is real domestic appreciation which has a negative effect on international competitiveness and thus on aggregate demand. This happened to Brazil in the 1990s when the Brazilian Real was pegged to the US Dollar but was allowed to crawl downwards in quantity notation. With a crawl rate below the difference between the Brazilian and the US inflation rate there was a significant real appreciation of the Brazilian currency, which damaged the Brazilian economy (Krugman and Obstfeld 2009, 477). In the EA, Germany experienced a decade of low nominal wage rises and inflation rates in the 2000s, alias known as real deprecation. This possibly damaged other EA member countries who accused Germany of wage dumping (Flassbeck and Spiecker 2011). The wage development in Germany itself, thus, can be interpreted as an asymmetric shock to other EA member countries (Flassbeck and Spiecker 2011; Bibow 2013). Relatively small wage increases in Germany yield real devaluation, stimulating German exports at the expense of other EA members whose competitiveness decreased as long as their wages increased faster.

Thus, potentially higher stabilization costs must be weighed against the promises of membership in a currency union, especially against the benefits of larger international trade and investment. As the stabilization cost argument is only valid in case of non-synchronized business cycles, we shall discuss the likeliness of business cycle synchronization in currency unions later in this chapter.

1.2 Aggregate Demand and Supply Shocks and the Financial Twist Argument

Membership itself might yield more synchronization endogenously, a variant of the seminal Lucas critique (Lucas 1976). In accordance, some authors favored the view not to use historical data to decide whether a country is suited for membership. Before we weight their arguments, however, we first have a look at a more pessimistic view on the viability of a common currency in the EU.

Authors like Bayoumi and Eichengreen (1993, 2017) emphasize the asymmetry argument and describe US regions as better suited for a currency union than the EA countries, although the United States is far from an OCA (Krugman 1993). Bayoumi and Eichengreen use real and nominal GDP data to calculate the real output growth (i.e., the first difference of the logarithm of real GDP) and inflation (i.e., the GDP deflator) for the eight US regions (as defined by the U.S. Bureau of Economic Analysis) and the 12 initial EU[2] members in their article from 1993. The same analysis was conducted by the authors in another article in 2017, where 11 initial EA members were studied. The data collected for the two articles ranged from 1963 to 1988 and from 1994 to 2014,[3] respectively. The correlations were only computed with respect to anchor regions, i.e., the Mid-East in the United States and Germany in the EA. Principal component analyses identified lower shares of variances of growth and inflation explained by the first principal component in the European countries in comparison to the US regions. Moreover, a bivariate VAR decomposition to distinguish temporary aggregate demand and permanent aggregate supply shocks found higher shock correlations for aggregate demand and aggregate supply in the US regions than in EA countries. This led the authors to their conclusion that the underlying causes for business fluctuations have been of a higher idiosyncratic nature in EA countries relative to US regions.

A closer look at Bayoumi and Eichengreen's arguments in their later work of 2017 is rewarding. They realigned the "core" and "periphery" dramatically in the EA whereas there were only minor changes in the United States. In the EA they identify a financial twist that reinforces aggregate supply and demand shocks.

The "core" is defined as a group of regions or countries that experience similar shocks. Whereas Germany (which is part of the core by definition), France and several Northern European countries formed the core in the EA previously (Bayoumi and Eichengreen 1993), it is now (Bayoumi and Eichengreen 2017) Germany and the GIIPS (Greece, Italy, Ireland, Portugal, and Spain) countries. They explained this realignment by an endogenous linkage of aggregate supply and demand through a financial twist. This way, they could explain price responses contrary to the canonical AS–AD model. The arguments of Bayoumi and Eichengreen (2017) are summarized in the following:

Usually, one expects a negative supply shock with increasing prices and decreasing output (see r.h.s. of Fig. 1) whereas a positive demand

[2] Formerly, it was the European Community, one of the predecessors of the European Union.

[3] They excluded the year 2009 as this year saw highly correlated shocks globally. This would bias the results according to the authors.

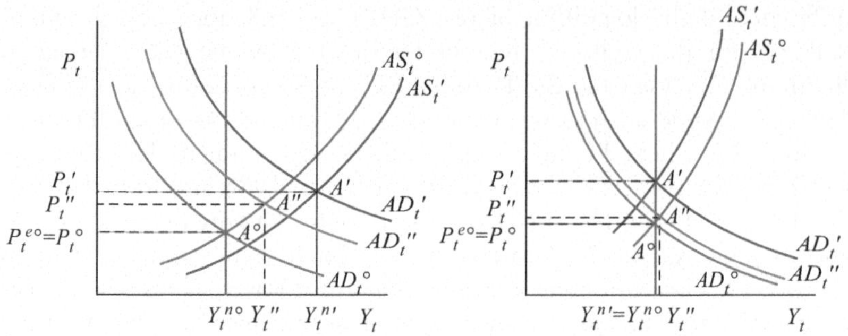

Fig. 4 Hysteresis in the AS–AD model in the EA, negative supply shock with demand response (l.h.s.), negative demand shock with supply response (r.h.s.) (*Source* Authors)

shock just leads to increasing prices (see l.h.s. of Fig. 1). A negative supply shock shifts aggregate supply upwards and becomes vertical in the long run leaving the economy with lower output and higher prices. A positive demand shock, to the contrary, shifts aggregate demand to the right, increasing output and prices. But, as aggregate supply rotates to be vertical again in the long run, prices increase further and output returns to its initial, natural level determined by the potential product of the economy.

In case of linked aggregate demand and supply curves, the canonical responses to shocks do not occur. This causes hysteresis. In the EA there was a credit boom before the financial crisis nourished by expectations of larger aggregate supply in peripheral EA members. Aggregate demand expanded together with investment, which increased aggregate supply initiating a self-fulfilling movement. In its aftermath the opposite happened (see the l.h.s. of Fig. 4), an expected negative aggregate supply shock in the Southern European countries lead to decreased aggregate demand (AD_t'') and aggregate supply eventually fell (AS_t°). This reinforced the decline of aggregate demand (AD_t°) and aggregate supply rotated to be vertical (left vertical line). As a result, prices fell and output declined to $Y_t^{n\circ}$. This way, they explained contracting output with falling prices.

There was another hysteresis in the EA: an aggregate negative demand shock to AD_t'' that is countered by wage restraint and austerity which shifts the aggregate supply curve downwards to AS_t° (see r.h.s. of

Fig. 4). This can even increase output temporarily despite the negative demand shock. As the output potential does not increase, aggregate supply rotates back to be vertical and a further lowering aggregate demand to AD_t° causes deflationary pressure.

The credit boom in Southern European countries coincided with the divergent price and wage developments (Flassbeck and Spiecker 2011) with effects on the competitiveness of EA members. Germany, on the one hand, started to keep wage increases below inflation and productivity gains in the 2000s, whereas in Southern European countries, on the other hand, the opposite happened. As unit labor costs drive prices, these dynamics seeded the later cause for macroeconomic imbalances in the EA. In the words of Flassbeck and Spiecker: "*[…] persistent divergences of inflation rates inside the monetary union are fatal because the differences in the cost and price level among the member countries accumulate over time and produce real exchange rate appreciation and depreciation, or, in other words, unsustainable over- and undervaluation for currencies that no longer exist*" (Flassbeck and Spiecker 2011, 181).

These specific problems challenge the common monetary policy and the coordination of fiscal policy in the EA. The potential macroeconomic impact of monetary policy, however, is restricted as consumers and firms usually do not suffer from money illusion, so that prices will adjust after a while.

2 Monetary Policy in the Euro Area—A Success?

We have seen that some scholars doubt that monetary policy in the EA can tackle the specific macroeconomic challenges of the Euro countries efficiently. But one shall first ask about the mandate of monetary policy. Its primary goal is price stability. Support to other aims of economic policy, such as increasing employment and sustaining economic growth, is secondary.[4] Price stability is reached in case of "*a year-on-year increase in the Harmonised Index of Consumer Prices for the EA of below 2%*" (ECB 2019a).

Flassbeck and Spiecker (2011) well-documented that—although the target inflation rate was met on average in the first decade of the Euro—there have been large disparities among EA members. Whereas the Southern European countries (fueled by the credit boom) experienced

[4] Article 127 Treaty on the Functioning of the European Union.

much higher inflation, Germany's price increases were way below the inflation target. In the aftermath of the financial crisis of 2007, the EA tumbled in a sovereign debt crisis that uncovered economic imbalances that openly questioned the very existence of the currency union.

In the summer of 2012, the ECB's president announced that "*within our mandate the ECB is ready to do whatever it takes to preserve the Euro*" (ECB 2012). Since then the central bank rates were lowered dramatically with the main refinancing rate down to 0.00%, the deposit facility rate negative with −0.40% and the marginal lending rate down to 0.25% since March 2016. In addition, longer-term refinancing operations have been launched, the fixed rate tender procedure with full allotment substituted the volume tender procedure with pro-rata-allotment and, most importantly, several asset purchasing programs have been implemented. The largest is known as the Quantitative Easing (QE) program which started in 2015, ended in 2018 and extended the ECB's balance sheet by roughly 2600 bn EUR. The asset purchasing program restarted at a reduced pace in November 2019. The deposit facility rate was further lowered to −0.50% in September 2019.

But why did the ECB follow the US FED and the Bank of England so late with its own QE program? According to De Grauwe (2018, 211) the late start was related to the fear of fiscal transfers in case of defaults shared by Northern EA countries.

Consequently, it was agreed that the ECB's program would be ministered by national central banks who only would purchase bonds of their own countries.[5] Moreover, the national banks only transferred 20% of these purchases to the ECB's balance sheet and kept 80% for themselves (De Grauwe 2018, 211–212). This procedure limits potential transfers as only 20% of the purchases are pooled (De Grauwe 2018, 212).

Core inflation has been positive the entire time and even trespassed the limit of 2% on two occasions (Fig. 5). In the last period of very low overall inflation rates, core inflation was close, but below the limit, as requested. Summarizing, the primary goal of monetary policy in the EA has been met, as core inflation has been below 2%, but positive.[6]

[5] The national countries' shares in the total amount of purchases equals their equity position in the ECB, e.g., 27.1% for the German Bundesbank (De Grauwe 2018, 211–212).

[6] If one looks at the asset price development, one cannot ignore the relationship between cheap money and soaring real estate prices in some EA member countries. Thus, if asset price inflation is accounted for, the ECB might have failed, but due to an over-expansionary monetary policy that in case of bursting bubbles endangers the secondary goal as well.

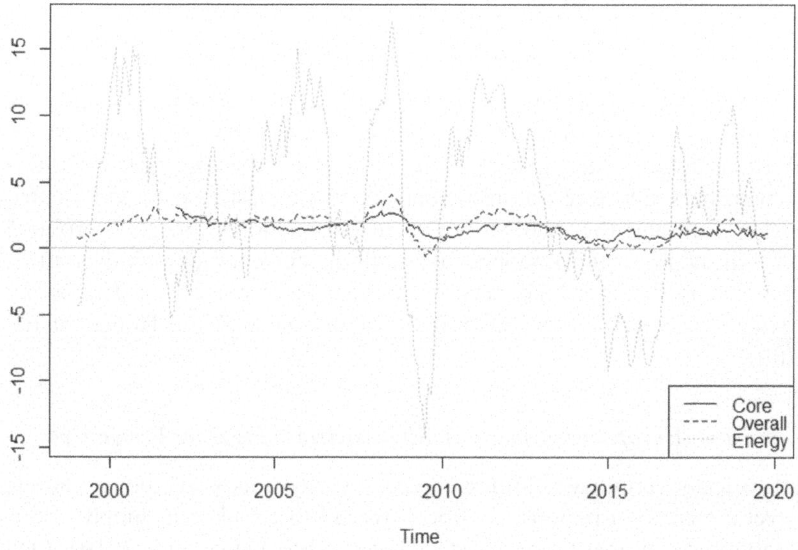

Fig. 5 Overall, core and energy price inflation in the EA from January 1999 to October 2019 (*Source* Authors [Eurostat])

On the other hand, quantitative easing clearly helped to further force interest rates to low levels and soften the burden of debtors, especially the sovereign ones. This way, the ECB hoped to stimulate aggregate demand, especially investment in the EA economies (ECB 2019b) and to buy EA member countries time to clean up their public finances and implement legislation that sets incentives for sustainable, long-term economic development.

Nevertheless, in Germany and Northern EA members, the argument that low interest rates are harmful to savers is brought forward frequently. It is, however, not convincing that the mandate of the central bank should guarantee a minimum interest rate. The question is whether the ECB's stabilization policy is suitable for all EA members or whether business cycles are too much apart such that a common policy is too costly.

3 The Possibility of Endogeneity in Business Cycle Synchronization

The view of endogeneity of the OCA criteria states that a currency union may evolve further to meet the optimal criteria simply by existing. Whereas Bayoumi and Eichengreen (2017) are rather skeptical about this view, others are more optimistic and identify a (faster) path to synchronization among the members of a currency union. Thus, the problem of asymmetry would disappear naturally in currency unions over time. One has to distinguish between results that are derived from data before (ex-ante perspective) and after (ex-post perspective) the launch of the Euro.

3.1 Europeanization and Globalization: Ex-Ante Perspective

Historically, regional business cycles usually followed the economic development of a regional anchor. International trade and supply chains established a global business cycle (Ductor and Leiva-Leon 2016). One asks, however, whether there is something like a genuine European business cycle. Artis and Zhang (1997) and Artis (2003) addressed this question. In their former work they showed that business cycle affiliation changed in Europe in the second half of the last century. Almost all countries that participated in the European Exchange Rate Mechanism (ERM)[7] changed their business cycle affiliation. Whereas their anchor country was the United States for the pre-ERM period before 1979, it became Germany for the post-ERM period. The only exception is the United Kingdom whose business cycle remained affiliated with the United States. These insights were drawn from monthly data on industrial production for 15 countries and over the period from 1961 to 1993.

Artis (2003) built on his earlier work and asked whether a genuine European business cycle evolved over time. He used quarterly GDP data and analyzed three subperiods, the two from Artis and Zhang

[7]The ERM started in 1979 and defined band widths within which nominal exchange rates were allowed to fluctuate. These band widths were relatively narrow with +/− 2.25% until 1992 and were increased in 1993 to +/− 15%. The ERM can be seen as a predecessor of the EA and was substituted by the ERM II, whose participation is mandatory for new EA members.

(1997) and, in addition, 1994 to 2000. For the two first subperiods the main finding of Artis and Zhang (1997) could be replicated, but the results for the last period are unclear with respect to the question asked. The cycles of Germany and the United States were highly correlated. Consequently, it does not make sense to speak of a genuine European business cycle. In Artis' words: "*The overall verdict is that it is quite hard to discern a homogenous or developing 'European cycle' with these data. Put loosely, globalization may be proceeding as fast as Europeanization*" (Artis 2003, abstract). The last twenty years the Chinese economy gained track and its dynamics impacted the economic development of its trading partners. Some observers even spoke of "Chimerica" in the light of the highly interdependent US and Chinese economies whose business cycle is correlated with the rest of the world (Ferguson and Xu 2018).

3.2 Higher Correlation in the EA: Ex-Post Perspective

There is empirical evidence that business cycles for EA member countries became more correlated over time as a consequence of membership. For example, Franks et al. (2018) used concordance statistics[8] and were able to show that business cycles have become more synchronized for the first 11 EA member countries.[9] They distinguished three subperiods[10] and considered the cyclical components of quarterly growth rates of real GDP. Besides, they considered negative, absolute GDP growth differentials. These increased in the latest subperiod which shows divergent amplitudes. De Grauwe (2018, 32) showed the same and stated that EA countries showed similar cycles but different intensities.

De Grauwe and Ji (2016) agreed and showed that business cycle synchronization, measured by the cyclical components of GDP growth,

[8] McDermott and Scott (2000) propose to measure the level of synchronization by calculating the fraction of time which two countries spend in the same cyclical phase. Thus, a statistic equal to one means that two countries have perfect positive concordance whereas one equal to zero means perfect negative concordance. The advantage is that, contrary to correlation, it cannot be biased by single large events that are common in two time series.

[9] EA-12 without Luxembourg.

[10] The period before the Euro, q1_1971 to q4_1998, the Euro era before crisis, q1_1999 to q1_2007, and the Euro era during and after the twin crises, q2_2007 to q1_2015.

was higher for the first 11 EA members[11] between 1995 and 2014. They partly explain the high correlation level in the EA by trade links. A simple OLS regression of bilateral correlation coefficients against the ratio of bilateral trade flows and the sum of GDPs of the respective countries only shows an R^2 of about 6%. Moreover, and in line with Artis (2003) they showed that business cycles among industrialized countries became highly correlated as well, but in a lower degree than among EA members. Usually, one explains the higher degree of correlation by interrelated exogenous financial shocks that hit all countries simultaneously. De Grauwe and Ji (2017) propose another and very convincing behavioral explanation. The rationality of economic agents is bounded so that shared narratives play an important role for decision-making under uncertainty. For example, an individual might take into consideration stories heard at the hairdresser's for taking investment decisions in the stock market. Consumers and investors, that drive aggregate demand, might share waves of optimism and pessimism, synchronizing their decisions. De Grauwe and Ji (2017) showed for a model of two countries that decisions do not rest on rational expectations but on simple heuristics, i.e., simple rules of thumb, self-fulfilling optimistic as well as pessimistic forecasts. The trade channel assures that these forecasts are transmitted to the economies of trading partners.

This argument strengthens the endogeneity argument for currency unions. In this case the same monetary policy and the storytelling associated to it favor sharing narratives interregionally and, consequently, business cycle synchronization. In contrast to traditional monetary policy which was supposed to be unpredictable to work, central banks today practice forward guidance. Future monetary policy is explained well in advance such that economic agents can build stable predictions. A strong contrast to Alan Greenspan, the FED's former chairman, who famously stated: "*If I've made myself too clear, you must have misunderstood me.*"[12]

This behavioral argument shall not be neglected when ascribing synchronization to larger interregional trade.

[11] EA-12 without Luxembourg.

[12] For more details, see https://www.independent.co.uk/news/business/if-ive-made-myself-too-clear-you-must-have-misunderstood-me-1328606.html.

Nota bene: Different authors use different measurements for asymmetry. The measurement of symmetry is important. One can measure bilateral correlations between the cyclical parts of real GDP, one can decompose GDP growth rates in a principal component analysis to identify the common underlying causes or one can compute concordance statistics. In addition, the negative absolute GDP growth differentials can be used to measure synchronization of business cycles. Whereas concordance statistics and correlations lead to the same qualitative result, the decomposition into shocks might lead to different ones.

We will follow the mainstream approach (*inter alia* Böwer and Guillemineau 2006) and measure business synchronization by bilateral correlations of the cyclical component of GDP. Cyclical components are extracted by applying the Baxter–King bandpass filter (see Baxter and King 1999). In Chapter 3, bilateral correlation coefficients across EA countries will be compared to those across US states. In addition, we will show their evolution in the EA since the 1960s as well as analyze those variables that determine them so that we can derive policy recommendations.

3.3 Determinant Variables of Business Cycle Synchronization in Currency Unions

It is disputed whether deeper economic integration yields more or less synchronized business cycles. It is, however, beyond controversy that the common European currency meant the latest and deepest step of economic integration for member countries.

To measure the impact of economic integration one identifies its dimensions and transmission channels. Afterwards, manifest variables that express these channels are measured and related to business cycle synchronization. Economic integration rests on minimal levels of trade barriers, financial integration and similarities in economic policies. It is uncontroversial that similar economic policies yield more synchronization of business cycles. In case fiscal and monetary policies have the same direction their impact on aggregate demand is expected to be the same. In the EA monetary policy is the same for all member countries and fiscal policies are restricted and thus "coordinated" through the European Fiscal Compact. It is less clear, however, how lower trade barriers and deeper financial integration work.

In case regions differ in their economic structure they are, *per definition*, exposed to idiosyncratic disturbances. Shocks in tastes and technologies affect more those regions that are specialized in the production of goods and services that served the former tastes or that are produced with the technologies affected. For example, the current ecological movement might change tastes of consumers with respect to their preferred power unit in cars or even their preferred means of mobility. This in turn could damage German carmakers that have a technological edge in the internal combustion engine, but not in electric motors. The car industry and their ecosystem of suppliers, on the other hand, are one of Germany's most important industries. It is, thus, a natural question to ask whether lower trade barriers and deeper financial integration increases or decreases economic specialization. Less business cycle synchronization is expected with higher specialization. Diversification, thus, is recommended for regions in a currency union as the risk of asymmetric economic shocks decreases with it. Therefore, it is optimal that all single regions or countries of a currency union have well-diversified economic structures (Kenen 1969).

Determinant Variables: Intra- and Inter-Industry Trade

Economically, it is important to learn whether lower barriers facilitate intra- or inter-industry trade. The former strengthens diversification whereas the latter yields specialization. Of course, higher intra-community trade can be expected from deeper economic integration through sharing a common currency as transaction costs are decreasing (see *inter alia* Rose et al. 2000; Frankel 2010). But, theoretically, both inter- and intra-industry trade can benefit from lower barriers.

According to the Heckscher–Ohlin model (Leamer 1995) trading regions specialize in the industries in which they have a comparative advantage due to a relative factor endowment that favors specialization. As a result, different regions specialize in different industries and engage in inter-industry trade. In contrast, intra-industry trade arises from love-for-variety preferences and monopolistic competition with increasing returns to scale (Helpman and Krugman 1985). This way, a common market for more regions increases and gives room to more varieties from the same industry at lower cost. The result is increased intra-industry trade.

Another strand of literature ascribes economic specialization to integrated financial markets, and, indeed currency unions, *per definition*, increase financial integration. Diversification of ownerships across several countries allows single countries to insure against idiosyncratic risk, with the result of economic specialization (Kalemli-Ozcan et al. 2001). The burden of unsystematic risk is partly carried by foreign investors and decreases the costs of economic specialization in a single country.

In the words of Kalemli-Ozcan et al. (2001): "*Financial integration will likely lead to more specialization since entrepreneurs will be less reluctant to 'put more eggs in the same basket.' This is because a greater fraction of their (or their investors') income will be derived from other sources, such as internationally diversified investment funds. Further, foreign investors will be buying shares in domestic firms since they themselves will be seeking to diversify their portfolios internationally. It is also likely that governments will insist less on subsidizing diversity within national borders.*"

Based on theoretical arguments, deeper economic integration can foster both more and less specialization. Consequently, we must answer the question empirically and measure the development of specialization in EA member countries. We follow Krugman (1993) who developed a specialization index, a distance measure, called the *Krugman Specialization Index (KSI)*. It is defined as the sum of absolute differences between the shares s of a region i in the different sectors k and the shares of region j in these sectors. Empirically, we measure these differences for T periods and take the average:

$$KSI_{ij} = \frac{1}{T} \sum_{t=1}^{T} \sum_{k} \left| s_{k,t}^{i} - s_{k,t}^{j} \right| \tag{1}$$

The *KSI* was much higher in US regions than in the main later EA members in the 1990 s, i.e., before the launch of the Euro. Therefrom, Krugman (1993) followed that the EA might await challenges for macroeconomic stabilization once the EA member countries follow their American peers and increase their economic specialization as a response to a common currency. In Krugman's words: "*Regional economies, being less diversified, are more subject to technology and demand shocks. This leads to a greater risk of severe region-specific recessions.*" Just as in the case of US regions—that are highly specialized—Krugman (1993) forecasted more regional specialization and instable regional exports in the EA due to lower transaction costs and external economies. This would lead to more asymmetry as regions with more specialization in their production structures have less correlated output fluctuations with other regions (*inter alia* Kalemli-Ozcan et al. 2001).

There are mixed empirical results with respect to the *KSI* in the EA. Whereas an early work discovered moderate evidence that specialization increased (Persson 2011), later work identified an increase of the unweighted *KSI*, even though some countries show decreased specialization and move toward the average of the first 12 EA members (Mongelli et al. 2016). In average, specialization in the EA[13] increased overall with the start of the Euro according to our data sample. The average *KSI* was 0.216 at the beginning of the EA (subperiod 1999–2002) whereas it increased continuously to 0.3267 in the last subperiod we consider (2011–2014).[14] Interestingly, for countries that are not both members of the EA, the average *KSI* increased from 0.337 to 0.444. Thus, the relative rise was smaller for pairs that are not both in the EA, even though for these pairs the distances in economic specialization are still much larger relative to those pairs of EA members.

Besides economic specialization exports and imports can be specialized. Trade specialization is thus proposed as an explanatory variable (Böwer and Guillemineau 2006). The trade specialization index *TSI* follows the Krugman specialization index. It is defined as the average sum of absolute differences between the export shares e of regions i and j in the different sectors k:

$$TSI_{ij} = \frac{1}{T}\sum_{t=1}^{T}\sum_{k}\left|e_{k,t}^{i} - e_{k,t}^{j}\right| \tag{2}$$

The average trade specialization index in the EA did not change considerably. It was, however, slightly higher during the years of the financial crisis and thereafter (5.007 in comparison to around 3.837 to 4.417).

Determinant Variables: Financial Integration

Financial integration plays a role beyond economic specialization. Its effects depend on the nature of the economic shock and were examined

[13] Our data sample comprises data for the 19 EA member countries, the other EU member countries, Norway and Switzerland. As the data covers data before the Brexit, the UK is accounted for as another EU member that does not share the Euro.

[14] We decomposed the entire period into four subperiods: 1999 to 2002, 2003 to 2006, 2007 to 2010, and 2011 to 2014.

closely by Cesa-Bianchi et al. (2016). In case of common shocks, financial integration leads to less synchronization, whereas in case of asymmetric shocks it yields more synchronization. This conclusion is intuitive as capital is assumed to flow to the regions with higher returns. Thus, in the case of a negative idiosyncratic shock in one region, capital should flow from the unaffected regions. Other work (*inter alia* Kalemli-Ozcan et al. 2013) proposed the opposite and show that financial integration leads to less synchronization.

Cesa-Bianchi et al. (2016) used negative absolute GDP growth differentials to measure business cycle synchronization and, just as GDP growth rates can be decomposed into responses to common and idiosyncratic shocks, they decompose the pairwise differences into a common and idiosyncratic component. The resulting three synchronization measures are regressed against bilateral bank linkages. Overall synchronization decreases with increased financial integration, but this is ascribed to common shocks as the idiosyncratic component of the synchronization measures is correlated positively with financial integration. Cesa-Bianchi et al. (2016) showed these relationships when using correlation coefficients and their decomposition as dependent variables.

Thus, again, these effects of financial integration are unclear and we have to measure financial integration empirically (Böwer and Guillemineau 2006). We add both outstanding bank assets a and liabilities l in the foreign country in relation to GDP, symbolized by y. The subscript ij indicates assets or liabilities of country i in or to country j.

$$CAP\_STOCKS_{ij} = \frac{1}{T}\sum_{t=1}^{T} log\left(\frac{a_{ij,t} + l_{ij,t}}{y_i} + \frac{a_{ji,t} + l_{ji,t}}{y_j}\right) \tag{3}$$

Due to data availability we cannot provide descriptive statistics for this variable's historical evolution.

Determinant Variables: Similar Policies

Frankel and Rose (1998) mentioned the spread of productivity shocks, but also of more coordinated policy shocks that might increase synchronization in currency unions. Indeed, currency unions tend to have similar economic policies through common institutions, common trade policies about extra-community trading partners and the agreement upon common guidelines or restrictions upon their national policies. Moreover, similar policies may propagate interregional waves of optimism and pessimism that are seen as the root for higher business cycle synchronization globally (De Grauwe and Ji 2017).

To measure similar policies in regions i and j the following distance variables are suggested (Böwer and Guillemineau 2006):

- The difference of real short-term interest rates ($RDIFF_{ij}$), calculated by deflating the short-term nominal interest rates, is used to capture the effects of different monetary policies:

$$RDIFF_{ij} = \frac{1}{T}\sum_{t=1}^{T} \left| r_{i,t} - r_{j,t} \right| \tag{4}$$

where $r_{i,t}$ is region $i's$ real short-term interest rate in period t.

- The difference of general government balances in relation to GDP ($DEFDIFF_{ij}$) is used to capture the effects of different fiscal policies:

$$DEFDIFF_{ij} = \frac{1}{T}\sum_{t=1}^{T} \left| d_{i,t} - d_{j,t} \right| \tag{5}$$

where $d_{i,t}$ is region $i's$ fiscal deficit relative to GDP in period t.
Within a currency union the differences in (4) are expected to be close to zero. This has been the case in the EA where interest rate spreads, short and long term, narrowed after the introduction of the Euro. During the sovereign debt crisis spreads for medium- and long-run rates widened again in the EA before the gap returned to much smaller levels in recent years. The narrowing interest rates are observed in our sample which shows an average difference of 1.957% in the first subperiod and 0.672% in the last. Differences became smaller outside the EA as well, down to 1.671% from 6.970%, but remain above EA levels.

Fiscal policies in the EA are bound by the intergovernmental fiscal pact of 2012. It limits structural deficit ratios to 0.5% of GDP, sharpening the limit of the allowed maximum of 3% agreed upon in the run-up to the Euro for all EU members. During the Euro's existence the deficit differentials have not narrowed further. The average differential was slightly higher in the third subperiod considered, the one covering the financial crisis and the years after. Besides, it is between 3.171 and

3.749%. Outside the EA there was little change as well, remarkably the average difference was slightly higher (4.415–4.815%).

Determinant Variables: Lower Trade Barriers
As long as lower trade barriers intensify inter-industry trade, less barriers lead to higher levels of specialization and a negative effect on business cycle synchronization. However, as outlined by Frankel and Rose (1998), common demand shocks and intra-industry trade can lead to the opposite. The two authors identified an overall positive effect of increased economic integration on business cycle synchronization for a panel of 20 industrialized countries for 30 years. Thus, even if the specialization channel was present, intra-industry trade and demand shocks were dominant.

In addition, trade facilitates research and development spillovers. According to Coe and Helpman (1995) a country's total factor productivity is affected by research and development pursued by its trading partners. The authors identified effects of both a country's domestic research and the development capital stock, as well as the research and development capital stocks of its trading partners. The effect of the foreign capital stocks is even larger for smaller countries. These knowledge spillovers promote business cycle synchronization. Different regions do not only interchange goods and services but also link the developments of their total factor productivities with each other.

The following measures are suggested for the effect of lower trade barriers (Böwer and Guillemineau 2006). It is convenient to use relative bilateral trade volumes, where trade volumes can be measured as a fraction of the total trade volume (BTT_{ij}) or of total GDP (BTY_{ij}) of the regions i and j, where x are exports, m imports, and y is GDP. In case of bilateral flows, the first letter in the subscript denominates the country and the second the destination or origin, respectively. Again, averages are used as measurements:

$$BTT_{ij} = \frac{1}{T}\sum_{t=1}^{T} \frac{x_{ij,t} + m_{ij,t} + x_{ji,t} + m_{ji,t}}{x_{i,t} + m_{i,t} + x_{j,t} + m_{j,t}} \tag{6}$$

$$BTY_{ij} = \frac{1}{T}\sum_{t=1}^{T} \frac{x_{ij,t} + m_{ij,t} + x_{ji,t} + m_{ji,t}}{y_{i,t} + y_{j,t}} \tag{7}$$

Average bilateral trade volumes measured as a fraction of total trade stayed constant during the Euro era. Average bilateral trade volumes relative to the trading partner's combined GDP, however, increased steadily from 0.009 in the first subperiod to 0.012 in the last subperiod. This increase illustrates the argument that international trade increased overall, not only intra-community trade, due to increased international labor division.

Trade openness generally is expected to have increased with the Euro. Overall trade openness (TTY_{ij}) can be measured as the average fraction of total exports and imports of the two countries and their respective GDPs:

$$TTY_{ij} = \frac{1}{T}\sum_{t=1}^{T} \frac{x_{i,t} + m_{i,t} + x_{j,t} + m_{j,t}}{y_{i,t} + y_{j,t}} \tag{8}$$

In fact, the average trade openness of EA countries increased considerably, since the adoption of the Euro, from 0.710 in the first subperiod to 0.857 in the last subperiod. Trade openness outside the EA is smaller, but increased, too, from 0.639 to 0.801.

A major advantage of a common currency is the abolition of exchange rate volatility, which reduces the need for risk-averse firms to hedge exchange rate risk. Consequently, inter-regional economic relationships shall increase, which might have an effect on business cycle synchronization. We measure exchange rate volatility by the variation coefficient, the ratio between the standard deviation and the average:

$$ER\_Vol_{ij} = \frac{\frac{1}{T-1}\sum_{t=1}^{T}\left(ER_{ij,t} - \frac{1}{T}\sum_{t=1}^{T} ER_{ij,t}\right)^2}{\frac{1}{T}\sum_{t=1}^{T} ER_{ij,t}} \tag{9}$$

There, $ER_{ij,t}$ is the exchange rate between two countries i and j in period t. Average volatility went down in the EA from 0.029 to 0.001. Some volatility still remains because EA members have not necessarily been members in the entire sample period leaving room for exchange rate fluctuations. Outside the EA fluctuations also decreased from 0.075 to 0.032. This might be due to outsiders who (at least temporarily) fixed their currencies to the Euro or that established a floor rate in quantity notation from the EA's perspective (Czech Republic, Denmark and Switzerland).

Economic Integration's Overall Effect

Returning to economic integration, there is no clear theoretical answer to the question whether it increases or decreases business cycle synchronization. Only similar policies yield definitely more synchronization for two different reasons: (1) because policies themselves constitute shocks and try to steer the economy and (2) because similar policies produce shared narratives among countries' economic agents and, thus, similar aggregate behavior. Tearing down trade barriers and deepening financial integration have ambiguous effects. Specialization, for example, reduces synchronization as the exposure to idiosyncratic shocks increases. On the other hand, demand or research spillovers increases synchronization. Table 1 summarizes the different effects of deeper economic integration for its three dimensions. The supposed impact on the respective channel is given by plus and minus signs, where a plus sign means that business cycles show a higher level of synchronization as a result. In the third column the variables used to measure the channels are stated.

Table 1 The effects of deeper economic integration on business cycle synchronization

Economic integration	*Channel*	*Variables*
More similar policies	• Policy coordination or common policies (+) • Animal spirits (+)	• Real interest rate differentials (Eq. 4), (−) • Government deficit rates differentials (Eq. 5), (−)
Less trade barriers	• Demand spillovers (+) • Animal spirits (+) • Specialization (−) • R&D spillovers (+) • Exchange rate uncertainty (?)	• Bilateral trade flows relative to GDP (Eq. 7), (+) • Bilateral trade flows relative to total trade (Eq. 6), (+) • Total trade flows relative to GDP (Eq. 8), (+) • Krugman specialization index (Eq. 1), (−) • Trade specialization index (Eq. 2), (−) • Exchange rate variation coefficient (Eq. 9), (?)
Deeper financial integration	• Specialization (−) • Idiosyncratic shocks (+) • Common shocks (−)	• Krugman specialization index (Eq. 1), (−) • Trade specialization index (Eq. 2), (−) • Bilateral capital stocks (Eq. 3), (?)

Source Authors

The signs in the variables' column indicate the supposed nature of the relationship with business cycle synchronization:

- With larger distances between real interest rates and government deficit rates, economic policies are less similar. Thus, we expect both variables to have a negative relationship.
- Increased bilateral trade flows, measured as fractions of GDP or total trade, as well as trade openness increase an economy's dependency on foreign demand. Thus, we expect a positive relationship for all three trade variables.
- Specialization increases vulnerability to idiosyncratic shocks. Thus, we expect both specialization variables to have a negative relationship.
- Lower exchange rate uncertainty increases bilateral trade volumes, but also might lead to higher specialization. Thus, the nature of the relationship is ambiguous.
- Higher bilateral capital stocks show deeper financial integration. Theoretically, the relationship is unclear and depends on the nature of the economic shock. In case of common shocks, the relationship is negative, otherwise positive.

Other Determinant Variables

There are other independent variables that influence the level of business cycle synchronization. Although nominal exchange rates are fixed in the EA, real exchange rates can adjust. Therefore, we consider real effective exchange rate differentials that measure regional competitiveness:

$$REFF\_ER_{ij} = \frac{1}{T}\sum_{t=1}^{T}\left|REFF\_ER_{i,t} - REFF\_ER_{j,t}\right| \tag{10}$$

There, $REFF\_ER_{i,t}$ is the real effective exchange rate index of country i, measured as the nominal effective exchange rate—i.e., measure of the currency values against a weighted average of several foreign currencies—divided by a price deflator. Average differentials decreased over time in the EA from 13.97 in the first subperiod to 3.15 in the last one indicating that gaps in competitiveness narrowed. We expect lower distances in competitiveness to increase business cycle synchronization as more similarity shall harmonize regions' abilities to react to economic shocks.

Moreover, it is straightforward to suppose that regions whose economic centers are further apart correlate less than regions that are closer to each other. The location of production is essential for bilateral trade volumes (Krugman 1991) and thus for business cycle synchronization. Despite its shortcomings we use the distance between two countries' capitals to measure their proximity. The capitals' distance is not undisputed as a gravity variable as capitals are not always a country's economic center or close to it. They can also be remote. A higher distance is assumed to decrease business cycle synchronization as it usually decreases the level of economic interaction (Böwer and Guillemineau 2006, 15). We call the distances between two capitals $DIST_{ij}$. Furthermore, the difference in two countries' populations relative to their combined population is assumed to explain synchronization.

$$POP_{ij} = abs\left(\frac{POP_{i,t} - POP_{j,t}}{POP_{i,t} + POP_{j,t}}\right) \tag{11}$$

Big differences reduce the overall importance of the economic relationship between the two countries making business cycles less synchronized (Böwer and Guillemineau 2006, 15). With respect to population differences, however, one can argue that the smaller economies tend to follow bigger ones so that significant differences in populations are correlated to more synchronized business cycles.

References

Artis, M. J. (2003). *Is There a European Business Cycle?* (CESIfo Working Paper, 1053).

Artis, M. J., & Zhang, W. (1997). International Business Cycles and the ERM: Is There a European Business Cycle? *International Journal of Finance Economics, 2,* 1–16.

Baxter, M., & King, R. G. (1999). Measuring Business Cycles: Approximate Band-Pass Filters for Economic Time Series. *Review of Economics and Statistics, 81*(4), 575–593.

Bayoumi, T., & Eichengreen, B. (1993). Shocking Aspects of European Monetary Unificaton. In F. Torres & F. Giavazzi (Eds.), *Adjustment and Growth in the European Monetary Union* (pp. 193–229). Cambridge: Cambridge University Press.

Bayoumi, T., & Eichengreen, B. (2017). *Aftershocks of Monetary Unification: Hysteresis with a Financial Twist* (IMF Working Paper, 17/55).

Bibow, J. (2013). The Euroland Crisis and Germany's Euro Trilemma. *International Review of Applied Economics, 27*(3), 360–385.

Blanchard, O. J., Eugenio Cerutti, E., & Summers, L. (2015). *Inflation and Activity: Two Explorations and Their Implications for Monetary Policy* (IMF Working Paper, 15/230).

Blanchard, O. J., & Katz, L. F. (1992). Regional Evolutions. *Brookings Papers on Economic Activity, 1,* 1–75.

Böwer, U., & Guillemineau, C. (2006). *Determinants of Business Cycle Synchronization Across Euro Area Countries* (ECB Working Paper, 587).

Cesa-Bianchi, A., Imbs, J., & Saleheen, J. (2016). *Finance and Synchronization* (CEPR Discussion Paper, 11037).

Coe, D. T., & Helpman, E. (1995). International R&D Spillovers. *European Economic Review, 39*(5), 859–887.

De Grauwe, P. (2018). *Economics of Monetary Union* (12th ed.). Oxford: Oxford University Press.

De Grauwe, P., & Ji, Y. (2017). The International Synchronisation of Business Cycles: The Role of Animal Spirits. *Open Economic Review, 28,* 383–412.

Ductor, L., & Leiva-Leon, D. (2016). Dynamics of Global Business Cycle Interdependence. *Journal of International Economics, 102,* 110–127.

Ferguson, N., & Xu, X. (2018). Making Chimerica Great Again. *International Finance, 21*(3), 239–252.

Flassbeck, H., & Spiecker, F. (2011). The Euro—A Story of Misunderstanding. *Intereconomics, 46*(4), 180–187.

Frankel, J. A. (2010). The Estimated Trade Effects of the Euro: Why Are They Below Those from Historical Monetary Unions among Smaller Countries? In A. Alesina & F. Giavazzi (Eds.), *Europe and the Euro* (pp. 169–212). Chicago and London: University of Chicago Press.

Frankel, J. A., & Rose, A. K. (1998). The Endogeinity of the Optimum Currency Area Criteria. *The Economic Journal, 108*(449), 1009–1025.

Franks, J. R., Barkbu, B. B., Blavy, R., Oman, W., & Schoelermann, H. (2018). *Economic Convergence in the Euro Area: Coming Together or Drifting Apart?* (IMF Working Paper, 18/10).

Helpman, E., & Krugman, P. (1985). *Market Structure and Foreign Trade: Increasing Returns, Imperfect Competition, and the International Economy.* Cambridge: MIT Press.

Kalemli-Ozcan, S., Papaioannou, E., & Peydró, J. L. (2013). Financial Regulation, Financial Globalization, and the Synchronization of Economic Activity. *Journal of Finance, 68*(3), 1179–1228.

Kalemli-Ozcan, S., Sørensen, B., & Yosha, O. (2001). Economic Integration, Industrial Specialization, and the Asymmetry of Macroeconomic Fluctuations. *Journal of International Economics, 55*(1), 107–137.

Kenen, P. (1969). The Theory of Optimum Currency Areas: An Eclectic View. In R. Mundell & A. Swoboda (Eds.), *Monetary Problems of the International Economy*. Chicago: University of Chicago Press.

Krugman, P. (1991). *Geography and Trade*. Cambridge: MIT Press.

Krugman, P. (1993). Lessons of Massachusetts for EMU. In F. Torres & F. Giavazzi (Eds.), *Adjustment and Growth in the European Monetary Union* (pp. 241–266). Cambridge: Cambridge University Press.

Krugman, P., & Obstfeld, M. (2009). *International Economics: Theory and Policy (International Edition)*. Boston: Pearson Addison-Wesely.

Leamer, E. (1995). *The Heckscher-Ohlin Model in Theory and Practice*. Princeton Studies in International Finance, 77.

Lucas, R. E. (1976). Econometric Policy Evaluation: A Critique. *Carnegie-Rochester Conference Series on Public Policy, 1*, 19–46.

McDermott, M., & Scott, N. (2000). *Concordance in Business Cycles* (IMF Working Paper, 00/37).

Mongelli, F. P., Reinhold, E., & Papadopoulos, G. (2016). *What's So Special About Specialization in the Euro Area? Early Evidence of Changing Economic Structures* (ECB Occasional Paper Series, 168).

Mundell, R. (1961). A Theory of Optimum Currency Areas. *The American Economic Review, 51*(4), 657–665.

Mundell, R. (1963). Capital Mobility and Stabilization Policy Under Fixed and Flexible Exchange Rates. *The Canadian Journal of Economics and Political Science/Revue Canadienne D'Economique Et De Science Politique, 29*(4), 475–485.

Persson, K. (2011). *Endogeneity and Specialization Theories of Optimal Currency Areas: A Comparative European Study* (Master thesis). Lund University.

Rose, A. K., Lockwood, B., & Quah, D. (2000). One Money, One Market: The Effect of Common Currencies on Trade. *Economic Policy, 15*(30), 7–45.

Internet Sources

De Grauwe, P., & Ji, Y. (2016). *Synchronisation in Business Cycles: An Endogenous Explanation*. Available at: https://voxeu.org/article/synchronisation-business-cycles Accessed February 3, 2020.

ECB. (2012, July 26). *Verbatim of the Remarks Made by Mario Draghi*. Speech by Mario Draghi, President of the European Central Bank at the Global Investment Conference in London. Available at: https://www.ecb.europa.eu/press/key/date/2012/html/sp120726.en.html. Accessed November 25, 2019.

ECB. (2019a). *The Definition of Price Stability*. Available at: https://www.ecb.europa.eu/mopo/strategy/pricestab/html/index.en.html. Accessed November 25, 2019.

ECB. (2019b). How Quantitative Easing Works. Available at: https://www.ecb.europa.eu/explainers/show-me/html/app_infographic.en.html. Accessed November 25, 2019.

CHAPTER 3

Empirics

Abstract This chapter performs two types of quantitative analysis: The first one is descriptive and studies correlations of GDPs as proxies for business cycles synchronization. We show that business cycles in the EA followed the international trend of increasing synchronization in the past decades but in a much higher intensity. This indicates that the EA itself has evolved toward more synchronization. Lately, synchronization decreased in the EA and globally. Moreover, EA business cycles seem to be stronger synchronized than in the United States. The second analysis of the chapter uses regressions of GDP correlations on the variables we described in Chapter 2, which are frequently associated to synchronization of business cycles by the literature. The idea is to check for the case of the EA the magnitude of association between those variables and synchronization.

Keywords Descriptive analysis · Regression analysis · Correlations of business cycles · Determinants of synchronization · Comparative analysis

This chapter presents the results for our empirical investigation of business cycle synchronization in the EA. In the first section we analyze correlations between the cyclical components of GDP of EA countries and compare them with those between US states. The second section compares correlations between EA countries with both those between

J. Kabderian Dreyer and P. A. Schmid,
Optimal Currency Areas and the Euro, Volume I,
https://doi.org/10.1007/978-3-030-46515-5_3

non-EA countries and between EA and non-EA countries historically. The third section presents the result of our regression analysis for different sample periods. The main objective of our regressions is to study the form and magnitude of the relationship between synchronization and the different independent variables that are expected to determine it as described in Chapter 2.

1 Business Cycle Synchronization in the EA and the United States

Globally, business cycles have become increasingly synchronized over the past decades. Despite the ambiguous role of deeper financial integration and inter-industry trade that fosters specialization, business cycles of industrialized countries more and more follow the same pattern. Nevertheless, EA member countries were regarded as ill-prepared for sharing the same currency in comparison to the United States because of the possibility of asymmetric economic dynamics. Some scholars even thought that the Euro would pave the path to disintegration or possibly secession from the EU. But one shall not forget: the United States consists of 50 single states and the District of Columbia that, too, experience different business cycles.

To compare the degree of business cycle synchronization in the EA to the one in the United States we gathered real quarterly GDP data from the first quarter of 2005 to the third quarter of 2018 for EU countries and for the US states and Washington, DC. Averages and variation coefficients of GDP correlations are displayed in the upper half of Table 1.

Table 1 Business cycle correlation, bilateral correlations

	European Union	*Euro area*	*United States*
Unfiltered real GDP (2005q1–2018q3)			
Mean	0.4954	0.5181	0.2979
Variation coefficient	0.4392	0.4424	0.8881
Filtered cyclical real GDP (2008q1–2015q3)			
Mean	0.6676	0.6401	0.4618
Variation coefficient	0.4081	0.4823	0.8668

Source Authors' own calculations

Notice that the mean correlation coefficient is much higher in the EU than in the United States. Moreover, EA members even show a slightly higher mean correlation coefficient than all EU members. The variation coefficient is highest in the United States followed by the EA and the EU.

We should, however, be interested only in cyclical components of GDP and thus follow Böwer and Guillemineau (2006) and apply the Baxter–King filter (Baxter and King 1999) on GDP series.[1] We prefer the Baxter–King relative to the Hodrick–Prescott filter because of its lower damage in case of the identification of spurious cycles (Woitek 1998). The overall picture is the same for cyclical components.

For all EU member countries as of 2017 the average bilateral correlation of the cyclical component is 0.6676 and the variation coefficient 0.4081. For the 50 US states and the District of Columbia the mean is much lower of 0.4618 and the variation coefficient higher of 0.8668. For the EA there is a slightly lower cyclical correlation on average than in the entire EU and a higher variation coefficient, but, again, the US states show considerably less average cyclical correlation and more variation than their EA counterparts.

The lower cyclical average correlation in the EA might be explained by the sovereign debt crisis in the currency union that has a relatively high weight. As the real economic impact of the sovereign debt crisis largely varied across EA members, a lower correlation is expected in the EA compared to the EU.

The higher overall correlation of real GDP is a hint. Dividing the total period into two subperiods (2008q1–2011q3 and 2011q4–2015q3) clearly shows that the average cyclical correlation decreased, and the variation coefficient increased, in the EU, the EA, and the United States. Moreover, synchronization among the initial eleven members of the EA, i.e., the countries that mostly[2] shared the common European market and its antecessors for decades, is highest, and variation lowest. But, although the sovereign debt crisis hit synchronization in these countries

[1]The extraction of cyclical components shortens the number of observations at the beginning and at the end by twelve quarters because these are needed for the decomposition. We set a lead and lag of 12 quarters to calculate the moving average. The lower limit is set to eight and the upper limit to 32.

[2]Austria and Finland joined the EU only in 1995.

Table 2 Business cycle correlation, filtered cyclical component, bilateral correlations

	European Union	*Euro area*	*Euro area 11*	*United States*
Subperiod 2008q1–2011q3				
Mean	0.7883	0.7820	0.9376	0.4735
Variation coefficient	0.4072	0.4585	0.0769	1.1549
Subperiod 2011q4–2015q3				
Mean	0.4192	0.4152	0.6226	0.3458
Variation coefficient	1.1417	1.1714	0.5935	1.3559

Source Authors' own calculations

intensively, it is still the highest among the different groups considered (see Table 2). Nonetheless, the variation coefficient increased and is higher in the EA than in the entire EU. For the eleven initial members, however, it is still the lowest. Compared to the United States, variation in the entire EA is still lower in the second subperiod.

> **Nota bene**: Average cyclical bilateral correlation is highest among the 11 initial Euro members, almost double in comparison to the United States. For all EA member countries it is still significantly higher than in the United States. But the decrease in the second subperiod was considerable and the variation coefficient was slightly higher in the EA than in the EU.

Some authors do not consider bilateral correlation coefficients but measure synchronization with respect to one anchor. Usually, Germany is taken as the anchor economy in the EU as well as in the EA. We respect this approach, but take the entire group's GDP as anchor variable. Large markets usually have more economic centers, and not one central star in the middle to which the others are related. Table 3 shows the same overall picture. Average correlation is highest for the initial eleven EA members and lowest for the United States. The reverse holds for variation: it is lowest for the initial eleven EA members and highest for the United States. In subperiod 2 means are lower and variation coefficients higher for all three groups.

Besides a comparison of European and US correlations, it is rewarding to have a look at the evolution of synchronization in the last decades in Europe. We turn to this analysis in the next subsection.

Table 3 Business cycle correlation, filtered cyclical components, correlations with entire currency union

	Euro area	*Euro area 11*	*United States*
Total period 2008q1–2015q3			
Mean	0.7870	0.8785	0.6617
Variation coefficient	0.3114	0.1485	0.4974
Subperiod 2008q1–2011q3			
Mean	0.8721	0.9667	0.6810
Variation coefficient	0.3419	0.0456	0.6784
Subperiod 2011q4–2015q3			
Mean	0.6392	0.7871	0.5195
Variation coefficient	0.5304	0.2982	0.7380

Source Authors' own calculations

2 The History of Business Cycles in Europe

We consider the evolution of business cycle synchronization in the EU and the EA. Therefore, we consider quarterly real GDP data from 1960q1 to 2018q3 and form three groups:

- Group 1: initial 15 members of the European Union as of 1995 (data available since 1960q1)
- Group 2: all group 1 members and the twelve Eastern European countries that joined the EU in 2004 and 2007 (data available since 1995q1)
- Group 3: all group 2 members and Croatia which joined the EU in 2013 (data available since 2000q1).

We compare the evolution internationally. For this purpose, we, additionally, look at three other groups:

- Group 4: Japan, Mexico, New Zealand, South Korea, United States, South Africa, Norway, and Switzerland (data available since 1960q1)
- Group 5: all group 4 members and Canada, Chile, Israel, Argentina, Indonesia, Russia, and Costa Rica (data available since 1995q1)
- Group 6: all group 5 members and India, Colombia, and Brazil (data available since 2000q1).

Table 4 Bilateral correlation coefficients, 1963q1–2015q3

	EA-11	*EA-12*	*EU-15*	*Group 4*
Mean	0.6357	0.5844	0.5613	0.3048
Variation coefficient	0.2832	0.3650	0.3512	0.9486

Source Authors' own calculations

Table 5 Bilateral correlation coefficients with group 4, 1963q1–2015q3

	EA-11	*EA-12*	*EU-15*
Mean	0.3286	0.3166	0.3134
Variation coefficient	0.5129	0.5446	0.5442

Source Authors' own calculations

Only the cyclical component of real GDP will be reported. Applying the Baxter–King filter again shortens the entire period considered by the first 12 and the last 12 quarters that are needed as lead and lag for the calculations of moving averages.

First, we look at bilateral correlation coefficients in the EA-11, in the EA-12, and in the initial 15 EU members together with the ones in group 4 (Table 4). In addition, we show the correlation coefficients of EA-11, EA-12 and EU-15 members with the countries of group 4 (Table 5). This shows that synchronization is much higher within the different European groups than internationally.

It is clear that synchronization is much higher in the EA and in the EU than among group 4 countries. Both the means are higher and the variation coefficients lower. Most synchronization is found among the initial eleven EA members.

International correlation outside the EA and the EU, is lower, indeed showing that synchronization is favored by proximity and by the common European market. To get an idea on how synchronization evolved over time we turn our analysis to 13 subperiods, each with 16 observations of cyclical components of quarterly real GDP. The first starts with 1963q4 and the last with 2011q4.

The overall pattern is the same in the EA-11, EA-12, EU-15, and in group 4 (see Fig. 1). The average correlation increased, and the variation coefficient of the correlation decreased. Recently, in the last subperiod from 2011q4 to 2015q3, however, the reverse happened. With

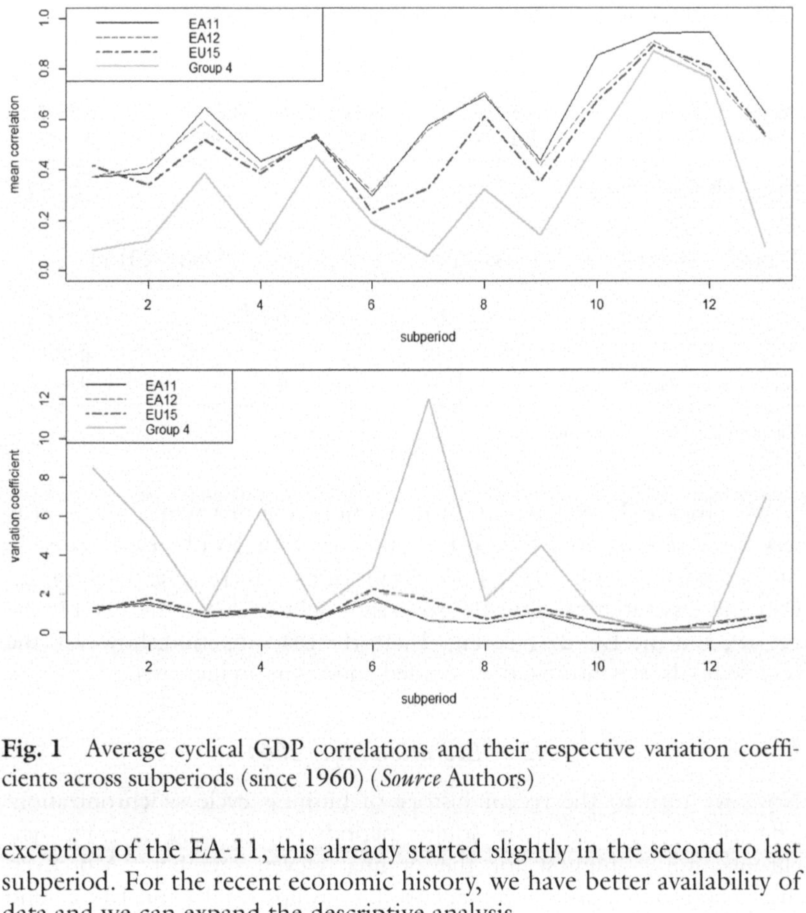

Fig. 1 Average cyclical GDP correlations and their respective variation coefficients across subperiods (since 1960) (*Source* Authors)

exception of the EA-11, this already started slightly in the second to last subperiod. For the recent economic history, we have better availability of data and we can expand the descriptive analysis.

2.1 Evolution Since 1995

We have a closer look for the time since 1995 (Tables 6 and 7).

Apparently, average business cycle synchronization is highest for the original 11 EA members, followed by the entire EA, by the EU and then by group 5. Variation is lowest for the EA-11 and highest for group 5. The original eleven EA members are even more synchronized with group 5 than those countries of EA-19 and EU-27.

Table 6 Bilateral correlation coefficients, 1998q1–2015q3

	EA-11	*EA-19*	*EU-27*	*Group 5*
Mean	0.8073	0.6504	0.6347	0.5552
Variation coefficient	0.1594	0.3633	0.3600	0.4443

Source Authors' own calculations

Table 7 Bilateral correlation coefficients with group 5, 1998q1–2015q3

	EA-11	*EA-19*	*EU-27*
Mean	0.5749	0.5164	0.5552
Variation coefficient	0.3551	0.4516	0.4443

Source Authors' own calculations

We observe five subperiods in the sample, the first with only 7 quarters from 1998q1 to 1999q3, the other six with 16 observations each, the last starting with 2011q4. We again can see increasing synchronization and less variation until the sovereign debt crisis for the EA-11, the EA-19, and the EU-27 (see Fig. 2). In the last subperiod, however, the reverse holds: synchronization receded and variation increased.

2.2 *Evolution Since 2000*

Now, we turn to the recent history of business cycle synchronization. The basic insights from the longer periods remain valid. Average synchronization is highest for the original eleven members. Moreover, there is not much difference between the groups EA-19 and EU-28 and countries of group 6 show the lowest average correlation. The variation among the EA-11 countries, again, is the lowest (Tables 8 and 9).

We divide the entire period into four subperiods, the first with only three quarters, the other three with 16 quarters each. The overall picture is unchanged (see Fig. 3). Average correlation increased over the first three subperiods and decreased in the latest one. The opposite holds for variation.

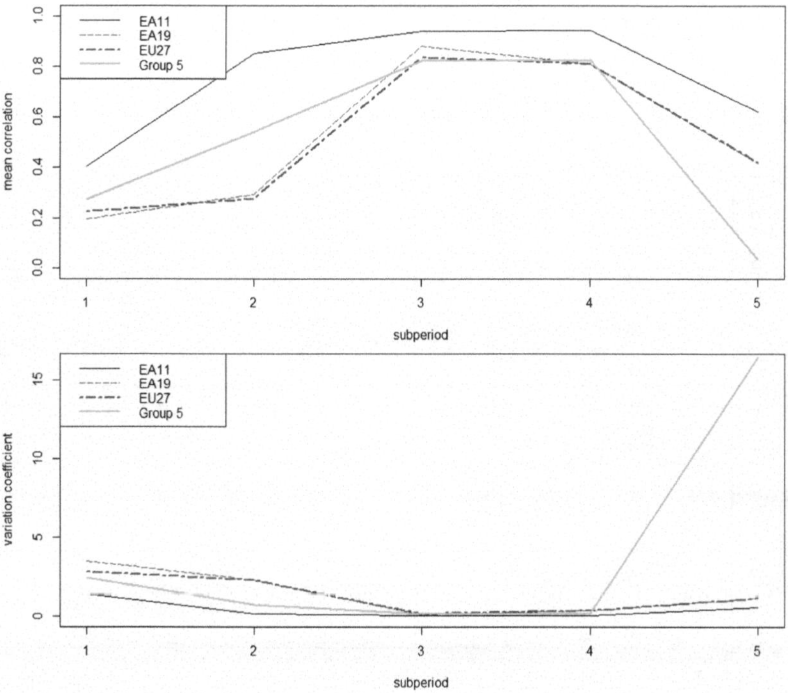

Fig. 2 Average cyclical GDP correlations and their respective variation coefficients across subperiods (since 1995) (*Source* Authors)

Table 8 Bilateral correlation coefficients, 2003q1–2015q3

	EA-11	*EA-19*	*EU-28*	*Group 6*
Mean	0.8194	0.7001	0.7050	0.6855
Variation coefficient	0.1668	0.3364	0.3007	0.2747

Source Authors' own calculations

Table 9 Bilateral correlation coefficients with group 6, 2003q1–2015q3

	EA-11	*EA-19*	*EU-28*
Mean	0.6714	0.6157	0.6166
Variation coefficient	0.2862	0.3940	0.3710

Source Authors' own calculations

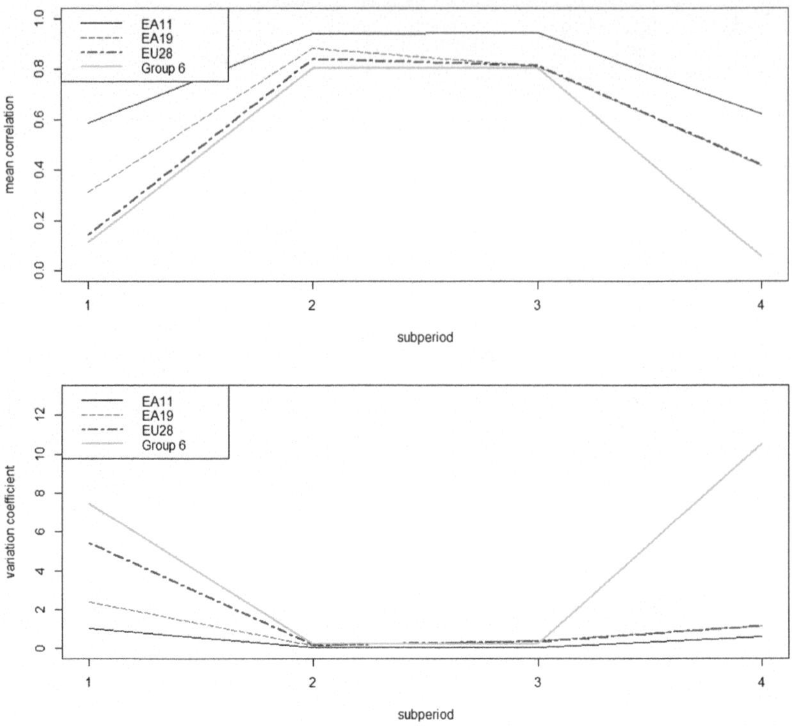

Fig. 3 Average cyclical GDP correlations and their respective variation coefficients across subperiods (since 2000) (*Source* Authors)

3 Key Variables for Synchronization

Synchronization between two countries proxied in this book by the correlation coefficients of their cyclical GDP components can be explained by a set of independent variables. Following Böwer and Guillemineau (2006) these are associated to specialization, trade barriers, similarity in economic policies, financial integration, competitiveness, and gravity measures. Lower trade barriers and more similar economic policies as well as competitiveness measures are expected to increase synchronization. The opposite is supposed for specialization, geographical distance, and similarity in population sizes. Moreover, the relationship between synchronization and financial integration is unclear.

Table 10 Estimation results for simple regression models

Independent variable	*Coefficient*	*Significance level*	R^2
KSI_{ij}	−0.05947		0.0076
TSI_{ij}	−0.01409	***	0.0529
$RDIFF_{ij}$	−0.02876	***	0.1557
$DEFDIFF_{ij}$	−0.01347	***	0.0442
BTT_{ij}	1.89474	**	0.0437
BTY_{ij}	2.68549	***	0.0497
TTY_{ij}	0.07147	.	0.0095
ER_Vol_{ij}	−0.51399	***	0.0528
$REFF\_ER_{ij}$	−0.00291		0.0058
$DIST_{ij}$	−0.00009	***	0.1865
POP_{ij}	0.07900	.	0.0120

Source Authors' own calculations
*** indicate a highly significant, ** very significant, * significant and . weakly significant coefficients

3.1 Estimations of Correlations for the Full Sample Period 1999–2014

Our data sample accounts for the period that starts with the Euro's introduction in 1999 and spans until 2014. Our estimations are based on Eq. (1):

$$\begin{aligned} COR_{ij} = \beta_0 + \beta_1 KSI_{ij} + \beta_2 TSI_{ij} + \beta_3 RDIFF_{ij} + \beta_4 DEFDIFF_{ij} + \beta_5 BTT_{ij} + \beta_6 BTY_{ij} \\ + \beta_7 TTY_{ij} + \beta_8 ER\_Vol_{ij} + \beta_9 REFF\_ER_{ij} + \beta_{10} DIST_{ij} + \beta_{11} POP_{ij} + \varepsilon_{ij} \end{aligned} \quad (1)$$

As data on capital stocks and flows is restricted and not available for the entire timespan, we decided to neglect financial integration at this stage and revisit an estimation setting with this variable later.

We start with simple regressions of correlations on each of these independent variables to check whether we find the expected signs for their coefficients when ignoring other control variables. This allows us to verify whether the estimation of the multiple model delivers robust coefficient estimates.

Table 10 provides the results for the estimations of our simple regressions. One can notice that the signs of the different slopes are as expected. Larger differences in population (*POP*) increase synchronization supporting our hypothesis that smaller countries follow the economic cycle of their larger pears or, in other words, the cycle of core

Table 11 Estimation results for the full model (3.1)

Independent variable	*Coefficient*	*Significance level*
KSI_{ij}	−0.05409	*
TSI_{ij}	−0.09900	***
$RDIFF_{ij}$	−0.04668	***
$DEFDIFF_{ij}$	0.09220	***
BTT_{ij}	−0.78732	
BTY_{ij}	0.17194	
TTY_{ij}	−0.01769	
ER_Vol_{ij}	0.72099	**
$REFF\_ER_{ij}$	−0.00790	**
$DIST_{ij}$	−0.00008	***
POP_{ij}	0.05101	
R^2	0.436	
$adj.R^2$	0.420	

Source Authors' own calculations
*** indicate a highly significant, ** very significant, * significant and . weakly significant coefficients

countries in the EA. Distances between countries (*DIST*), however, decrease correlation. Thus, the two gravity variables turn out to have the supposed impact. All three trade variables (BTT, BTY, TTY) are associated to an increase in correlations, while the opposite is valid for the two variables that measure distance in economic policies (*RDIFF*, *DEFDIFF*). These results support the hypothesis that the same policy shocks and trade relations synchronize business cycles. Specialization (*KSI*, *TSI*), however, which is the result of international labor division counteracts this synchronization effect. The same holds for the volatility in exchange rates (*ER_Vol*). The distance in real effective exchange rates has the supposed sign, but is not significant. Thus, we find no support for a relationship between distance in competitiveness and business cycle synchronization.

Now, we turn to model (3.1) whose estimation results are given in Table 11.

Prima vista the estimation results for the full model could be seen as a paradox, as some signs of coefficients changed in comparison to those we find when running simple regressions. There are two variables that have coefficients that inverted signs compared to the simple regressions and are even statistically significant, i.e., distances in government deficits and exchange rate volatility. For bilateral trade volumes relative to GDP and trade openness, the signs are unexpected (also inverted), but—at least—not significant. But why should countries whose fiscal policies diverge and whose exchange rate fluctuates more intensively enjoy more synchronization? We would expect the opposite because similar policies should evoke similar economic responses and consequently be associated to less variation among business cycles. As a result of similar policies, the risk in the economic relationship between two countries should be reduced. Moreover, for trade variables, coefficient signs should not be negative as more trade and openness are expected to promote the alignment of business cycles. To put it simply, these estimates are contrary to economic intuition and do not make sense. Furthermore, many variables lose significance. One can observe that four variables cannot be considered significant in (3.1). Thus, there is an indication of inflation of variance in the model. Inflated variances yield higher denominators in the inference tests (t-scores) and increase the possibility of a type II error. Multicollinearity among independent variables might be the reason for this problem. Thus, in this case some independent variables should not be used together to explain business cycle synchronization. Possible problems could be linked to the following independent variables:

- The two trade variables *BTT* and *BTY* measure trade intensity and thus using both variables in a model could be redundant;
- Trade specialization is the result of higher trade intensity based on inter-industry trade;
- Geographical proximity likely increases trade intensity;
- Fiscal and monetary policies, often, are interrelated as both fiscal and monetary instruments usually try to tune business cycles;
- Differences of interest rates and exchange rate volatility are related via the interest rate parity hypothesis.

The variance inflation factor (*VIF*) formally checks these problems by regressing "independent on independent" variables. Thus, the higher the *VIF*, the higher the variance of a single independent variable that is explained by the other independent variables, i.e., a *VIF* of 2 states that half of the variance of an independent variable is explained by the other independent variables. Table 12 summarizes the *VIF*-analysis. In the

Table 12 VIF analysis for model (3.1)

Model	*Model (3.1)*		*w/o* TSI_{ij}		*w/o* BTY_{ij}		*w/o* R_DIFF_{ij}		*w/o* $DIST_{ij}$
Variable	*Coefficient (standard error)*	*VIF*	*Coefficient (standard error)*	*VIF*	*Coefficient (standard error)*	*VIF*	*Coefficient (standard error)*	*VIF*	*Coefficient (standard error)*
KSI_{ij}	−0.05408 (0.02587)*	1.13	−0.06484 (0.02650)*	1.12	−0.06493 (0.02648)*	1.12	−0.01555 (0.03267)	1.07	0.00407 (0.04314)
TSI_{ij}	−0.09900 (0.02374)***	119.16							
$RDIFF_{ij}$	−0.04668 (0.00546)***	4.08	−0.04811 (0.00594)***	4.07	−0.04807 (0.00594)***	4.06			
$DEFDIFF_{ij}$	0.09219 (0.02479)***	119.42	−0.01105 (0.00218)***	1.09	−0.01102 (0.00217)***	1.09	−0.01028 (0.00248)***	1.09	−0.01087 (0.00318)***
BTT_{ij}	−0.78732 (0.99166)	8.06	−0.80521 (0.98845)	8.06	−0.55124 (0.46086)	1.46	−0.17775 (0.51634)	1.44	1.88439 (0.56471)***
BTY_{ij}	0.17194 (0.97274)	7.66	0.36371 (0.95270)	7.65					
TTY_{ij}	−0.01769 (0.03194)	1.67	−0.03555 (0.03252)	1.64	−0.03080 (0.02948)	1.29	−0.00787 (0.03229)	1.28	0.09477 (0.03846)*
ER_Vol_{ij}	0.72099 (0.22519)**	5.03	0.76404 (0.23699)**	5.01	0.76368 (0.23674)**	5.01	−0.64971 (0.11593)	1.27	−0.56747 (0.12997)***
$REFF\_ER_{ij}$	−0.00790 (0.00255)**	1.60	−0.00844 (0.00265)**	1.59	−0.00846 (0.00265)**	1.59	−0.00158 (0.00204)	1.29	0.00141 (0.00197)
$DIST_{ij}$	−0.00008 (0.00001)***	1.50	−0.00009 (0.00001)***	1.48	−0.00009 (0.00001)***	1.48	−0.00010 (0.00001)***	1.47	
POP_{ij}	0.05101 (0.03176)	1.26	0.01764 (0.03153)	1.16	0.01841 (0.03136)	1.15	0.04888 (0.03522)	1.14	0.10600 (0.03880)**
R^2	0.435		0.414		0.414		0.307		0.1628
$adj.R^2$	0.420		0.399		0.400		0.292		0.1481

Source Authors' own calculations

In the first line the estimated coefficients are given, in the second the standard errors. *** indicate a highly significant, ** very significant, * significant and . weakly significant coefficient first column the *VIFs* for model (3.1) are given. In the second to fifth columns variables are removed step-by-step and regression coefficients, standard errors, and *VIFs* are given.

Both trade specialization and deficit differentials are explained to a great extent by the remaining independent variables (*VIFs* > 100). Consequently, we remove trade specialization and recalculate the *VIFs* in the second column. Here we can notice that both *VIFs* associated to variables that measure bilateral trade intensity *BTT* and *BTY* are high (*VIFs* > 7). Thus, we remove the variable associated to bilateral trade volumes relative to GDP (*BTY*) in the estimations of the third column. In this case, exchange rate volatility and real interest rate differentials are both explained by the remaining variables (*VIFs* > 4). So we continue in column 4 without considering differences in real interest rates as independent variable.

Finally, the signs of *BTT* and *TTY* are both negative, contrary to what we expect according to economic theory. As geographical distance discourages trade, distance and trade variables should not be used together as explaining variables. This leaves us with a model that considers economic specialization, bilateral trade volumes, trade openness, deficit differentials, exchange rate volatility, and population gravity as regressors. Thus, when running our multiple regressions, four rules are established:

- Trade specialization and deficit differentials should not be used in the same model;
- Bilateral trade volumes, *BTT* and *BTY*, should not be used together;
- Interest rate differentials and exchange rate volatility should not be used in the same model;
- Geographical distance and trade variables should not be used in the same model.

Based thereon, we define the twelve multiple regression models of Table 13, where a check mark indicates that the respective variable is used as regressor.

In order to analyze estimation results of the models described in Table 13, we try to identify the combination of independent variables for each model that yields the highest "statistical quality." In order to do so, using R^2 would not be recommendable since it increases according to the number of independent variables added. One could overcome this problem by using the adjusted R-squared. However, the *AIC*

Table 13 Multiple regression models

Variable/Model	*A*	*B*	*C*	*D*	*E*	*F*	*G*	*H*	*I*	*J*	*K*	*L*
KSI_{ij}	✓	✓	✓	✓	✓	✓	✓	✓	✓	✓	✓	✓
TSI_{ij}					✓	✓	✓	✓			✓	✓
$RDIFF_{ij}$			✓	✓			✓	✓		✓		✓
$DEFDIFF_{ij}$	✓	✓	✓	✓					✓	✓		
BTT_{ij}	✓		✓		✓		✓					
BTY_{ij}		✓		✓		✓		✓				
TTY_{ij}	✓	✓	✓	✓	✓	✓	✓	✓				
ER_Vol_{ij}	✓	✓			✓	✓			✓		✓	
$REFF\_ER_{ij}$	✓	✓	✓	✓	✓	✓	✓	✓	✓	✓	✓	✓
$DIST_{ij}$									✓	✓	✓	✓
POP_{ij}	✓	✓	✓	✓	✓	✓	✓	✓	✓	✓	✓	✓

Source Authors' own calculations

likelihood criterion is regarded as superior. It also penalizes adding extra independent variables to the model. Thus, we use the *AIC* for model selection. The same would be valid if we would have chosen the *BIC* (Schwartz criterion), which would only change results marginally.

In addition, we would also like to find out whether EA membership impacts business cycle synchronization. As many of the independent variables we use could be considered channels through which EA membership operates to increase correlations, the addition of just an EA membership variable will probably not yield the information we search for. In other words: what effect is left for EA membership if we control for the different channels through which the EA impacts synchronization? Consequently, we decide to add a 13th model M with an EA membership variable. First, membership length is normalized to the intervall [0,1]. Second, the membership variable is calculated as the product of membership lengths for two countries. In addition, model M ignores all independent variables except for the two gravity ones. These are, by definition, not affected by membership, but play a role for synchronization as neighboring countries and countries with population differences are expected to be more synchronized than those that lie farther apart and/or have similar population sizes.

Estimation results for the 13 models, i.e., the 12 from Table 13 (A–L) and one accounting for EA membership (M), are given in Tables 14 and 15. Please note, that we only report those results for independent variables that are chosen based on the *AIC* criterion and thus maximize

Table 14 Estimation results multiple regressions models A–H for entire period

Variable/ Model	*A*	*B*	*C*	*D*	*E*	*F*	*G*	*H*
KSI_{ij}	–	–	–	–	–	–	–	–
TSI_{ij}	–	–	–	–	−0.01182	−0.01220	−0.01213	−0.01242
					(0.00341)***	(0.00341)***	(0.00329)***	(0.00328)***
$RDIFF_{ij}$	–	–	−0.02810	−0.02838	–	–	−0.02815	−0.02840
			(0.00302)***	(0.00300)***			(0.00298)***	(0.00297)***
$DEFDIFF_{ij}$	−0.01104	−0.01145	−0.01143	−0.01175	–	–	–	–
	(0.00325)***	(0.00325)***	(0.00314)***	(0.00313)***				
BTT_{ij}	1.86085	–	1.60786	–	1.80086	–	1.54876	–
	(0.57942)**		(0.53025)**		(0.58003)**		(0.52988)**	
BTY_{ij}	–	2.34706	–	2.07149	–	2.27163	–	1.99750
		(0.70282)***		(0.64849)**		(0.69883)**		(0.64311)**
TTY_{ij}	0.09021	0.05603	0.08808	–	0.08795	0.05490	0.08600	0.05741
	(0.03819)*	(0.04133)	(0.03529)*		(0.03839)*	(0.04158)	(0.03547)*	(0.03807)
ER_Vol_{ij}	−0.53135	−0.53649	–	–	−0.53484	−0.53979	–	–
	(0.11517)***	(0.11504)***			(0.11473)***	(0.11458)***		
$REFF\_ER_{ij}$	–	–	–	–	–	–	–	–
$DIST_{ij}$	–	–	–	–	–	–	–	–
POP_{ij}	0.10534	0.09728	0.08875	0.08198	0.10661	0.09894	0.09019	0.08379
	(0.03807)**	(0.03836)*	(0.03490)*	(0.03490)*	(0.03800)**	(0.03827)*	(0.03474)**	(0.03472)*
R^2	0.161	0.158	0.251	0.250	0.168	0.165	0.258	0.257
$adj.R^2$	0.151	0.147	0.242	0.241	0.158	0.155	0.249	0.248
AIC	−1307.4	−1305.7	−1353.5	−1352.8	−1310.8	−1309.2	−1357.3	−1356.7

Source Authors' own calculations
In the first line the estimated coefficients are given, in the second the standard errors. *** indicate a highly significant, ** very significant, * significant and . weakly significant coefficients

Table 15 Estimation results multiple regressions models I–M for the entire period

Variable/Model	*I*	*J*	*K*	*L*	*M*
KSI_{ij}	−0.01195	−0.02994	−0.01059	−0.02864	–
	(0.03215)	(0.02629)	(0.03192)	(0.02613)	
TSI_{ij}			−0.01054	−0.01089	–
			(0.00251)***	(0.00242)***	
$RDIFF_{ij}$		−0.02845		−0.02845	–
		(0.00248)***		(0.00247)***	
$DEFDIFF_{ij}$	−0.01003	−0.01048			–
	(0.00247)***	(0.00240)***			
BTT_{ij}	–	–	–	–	–
BTY_{ij}	–	–	–	–	–
TTY_{ij}	–	–	–	–	–
ER_Vol_{ij}	−0.68303		−0.68422		–
	(0.10324)***		(0.10328)***		
$REFF\_ER_{ij}$	–	−0.00401	–	−0.00401	–
	–	(0.00181)*	–	(0.00180)*	–
$DIST_{ij}$	−0.00009	−0.00009	−0.00009	−0.00009	−0.00009
	(0.00001)***	(0.00001)***	(0.00001)***	(0.00001)***	(0.00001)***
POP_{ij}	0.05218	0.04028	0.05471	0.04299	0.05176
	(0.03328)	(0.03013)	(0.03324)	(0.03009)	(0.03624)
EA	–	–	–	–	0.12745
					0.03087***
R^2	0.305	0.388	0.310	0.393	0.240
$adj.R^2$	0.296	0.379	0.302	0.384	0.234
AIC	−1383.6	−1433.5	−1386.5	−1436.6	

Source Authors' own calculations
In the first line the estimated coefficients are given, in the second the standard errors. *** indicate a highly significant, ** very significant, * significant and . weakly significant coefficients

the goodness-of-fit of our estimations. The main findings for the chosen configurations are:

Specialization Variables
Although economic specialization is not significant in any model, trade specialization has a significant and negative relationship with business cycle synchronization. This confirms that countries with higher trade specialization are more vulnerable to idiosyncratic shocks. If two economies rely on specific sectors that are different, business cycles may follow distinct patterns.

Policy Variables
For the two policy variables, distances in real interest rates and fiscal deficits, we identify significant negative relationships. We confirm that distances in policies are associated with less synchronization. This is economically intuitive as distinct policies should have differing effects on aggregate demand and thus on business cycle dynamics.

Trade Variables
There are two bilateral trade variables: bilateral trade volumes as a fraction of total trade and as a fraction of total GDP. Both have a positive relationship with synchronization. Higher trade intensity increases synchronization. This indicates the importance of intra-industry trade where two economies rely on the same industries.

In addition, trade openness measured by the fraction of two economies' total trade in relation to their combined GDPs is positively related to their degree of synchronization. Openness means that the global economic dynamic has a greater influence on both countries and thus leads to a higher level of synchronization.

Exchange Rates
The volatility of the nominal exchange rate is negatively related to synchronization. This is intuitive because the higher the volatility, the higher the transaction costs.

The real effective exchange rate is usually taken as a competitiveness measure. Distances in effective rates are only viable (selected based on *AIC* and statistically significant) in two cases. There, the relationship is negative and shows that larger gaps in competitiveness decrease business cycle synchronization. The small number of significant coefficients might be caused by the long-term nature of the sample. Distances in real effective rates can theoretically only persist in the short run, given price rigidities.

Gravity Variables
The two gravity variables, geographical distance and population, have opposite sings. Whereas proximity increases, similarity in population sizes decreases correlations of business cycles. In case two countries are farther away from each other, their relationship is expected to be weaker and business cycles less correlated. On the other hand, one should expect small countries to follow the economic development of their larger neighbors.

The gravity variables are also used in the additional model M that explores the role of EA membership in synchronization. Once again, geographical distance plays a negative role, i.e., it decreases correlation, while there is no evidence for an impact of population size.

EA Membership
EA membership is positively related to business cycle correlation and this relationship is statistically significant. This shows a positive role of the common currency for synchronization. Note again, that one should not include variables such as those referring to specialization, economic policies, trade, and exchange rates in this estimation as they could be seen as "transmission channels" of EA membership.

3.2 Estimations for Four Subperiods from 1999 to 2014

We can divide the period between 1999 and 2014 into four phases of the EA's evolution. The early years from 1999 to 2002 are considered the launch of the common currency and, also those leading to the burst of the dotcom bubble. The second subperiod from 2003 to 2006 constitutes the run-up to the financial crisis and can be seen as "calm" years for stabilization policies. Then, in 2007 the housing bubble in the United States burst leading to economic repercussions in all industrialized countries of the West, including EA members. This subperiod includes 2007 and the following years until 2010 that experienced the immediate aftermath of the financial crisis. Thereafter, a sovereign debt crisis followed with severe effects for some EA countries, culminating in the famous "Whatever-it-takes" speech of the ECB's former president Mario Draghi in the summer of 2012. This event is part of the last subperiod from 2011 to 2014.

Technically, we have four subperiods of data, so that our sample does not consist any longer of cross-sectional, but of panel data. We use the same independent variables as previously according to the regression model (3.2):

$$\begin{aligned} COR_{ij,t} = \beta_0 + \beta_1 KSI_{ij,t} + \beta_2 TSI_{ij,t} + \beta_3 RDIFF_{ij,t} + \beta_4 DEF\_DIFF_{ij,t} + \beta_5 BTT_{ij,t} + \beta_6 BTY_{ij,t} \\ + \beta_7 TTY_{ij,t} + \beta_8 ER\_Vol_{ij,t} + \beta_9 REFF\_ER_{ij,t} + \beta_{10} DIST_{ij} + \beta_{11} POP_{ij,t} + \varepsilon_{ij,t} \end{aligned} \quad (2)$$

As for the entire period we neglect financial integration in the analysis of subperiods due to data availability and will consider capital stocks as independent variable later in this study. The analysis of panel data suggests the application of different techniques. One can either pool the data together or use the so-called fixed or random effects approaches (see Dreyer and Schmid 2015). Econometrically, it would be hard to imagine a specific effect of the different country pairs on estimations. This would imply that a combination of two countries alone would affect correlations irrespective of the different control variables used. Thus, we chose to apply the pooling method alongside subperiod dummy variables that account for the specific time-related effects. We use the first subperiod as base level.

This section follows the same structure that was used in the analysis of the entire period. We start with simple regressions, use *VIFs* to extract the variables of interest and choose sets of independent variables that best explain business cycle correlations based on the *AIC* criterion. Table 16 summarizes the results for the simple regressions.

A higher difference in populations should increase business cycle synchronization as smaller countries tend to follow the economic cycles of larger ones. Thus, the estimated sign for the coefficient related to population gravity is expected, even though it is not any longer statistically significant. There is no change with respect to geographical distance: It is still significant and lowers bilateral correlations. The same holds for the specialization variables: trade specialization has a negative and significant coefficient, while no significance is found for economic specialization. The signs for differences in interest rates, deficits, real effective exchange rates and for exchange rate volatility are as expected and statistically significant.

Table 16 Estimation results for simple regression models including time dummies for subperiods

Variable	*Coefficient Standard error*	*2006 Standard error*	*2010 Standard error*	*2014 Standard error*	R^2
$KSI_{ij,t}$	−0.05223	0.01765	0.48370	0.04656	0.1613
	(0.04770)	(0.03236)	(0.02954)***	(0.03099)	
$TSI_{ij,t}$	−0.01429	0.01595	0.49458	0.04307	0.1728
	(0.00243)***	(0.03076)	(0.02637)***	(0.02874)	
$RDIFF_{ij,t}$	−0.02255	−0.04777	0.41282	−0.03914	0.1973
	(0.00259)***	(0.03459)	(0.02938)***	(0.03928)	
$DEFDIFF_{ij,t}$	−0.01346	0.01577	0.49403	0.04284	0.1706
	(0.00250)***	(0.03071)	(0.02639)***	(0.02899)	
$BTT_{ij,t}$	2.79075	0.01389	0.47721	0.03918	0.1780
	(0.40891)***	(0.03483)	(0.02880)***	(0.03928)	
$BTY_{ij,t}$	3.30015	0.01174	0.47281	0.02984	0.1740
	(0.56945)***	(0.03508)	(0.02892)***	(0.03952)	
$TTY_{ij,t}$	−0.00190	0.01600	0.48064	0.04253	0.1600
	(0.05516)	(0.03256)	(0.03020)***	(0.03157)	
$ER\_Vol_{ij,t}$	−2.05517	−0.04599	0.45021	−0.03334	0.1929
	(0.22377)***	(0.03444)	(0.02848)***	(0.03880)	
$REFF\_ER_{ij,t}$	−0.01223	−0.02691	0.36565	−0.09022	0.1944
	(0.00190)***	(0.03154)	(0.03027)***	(0.03366)**	
$DIST_{ij}$	−0.00004	0.01593	0.48050	0.04223	0.1672
	(0.00001)**	(0.03234)	(0.02980)***	(0.03004)	
$POP_{ij,t}$	0.041611	0.01592	0.48052	0.04226	0.1608
	(0.046978)	(0.03222)	(0.02901)***	(0.02999)	

Source Authors' own calculations

*** indicate a highly significant, ** very significant, * significant and . weakly significant coefficients

An explanation for the change in significance of the coefficient related to the difference in real effective exchange rates in the subperiod analysis could be the short-term rigidity in prices. For the entire period, gains in competitivity achieved through devaluations of real exchange rates are not sustainable, as they are compensated with inflation (prices should be expected to fluctuate and adjust devaluations in real exchange rates). This should not happen in the short term, when prices are rigid. Thus, even though it would be natural to observe a significant coefficient associated to differences in real exchange rates in the short term, this is not true for the long term.

Table 17 Estimation results for the full model (3.2)

Variable	*Coefficients*	*Significance*
Intercept	0.77750	***
$KSI_{ij,t}$	0.00724	
$TSI_{ij,t}$	–0.10747	***
$RDIFF_{ij,t}$	−0.01548	***
$DEFDIFF_{ij,t}$	0.09908	**
$BTT_{ij,t}$	1.56240	
$BTY_{ij,t}$	−0.35022	
$TTY_{ij,t}$	−0.04620	
$ER\_Vol_{ij,t}$	−0.54463	
$REFF\_ER_{ij,t}$	−0.01136	***
$DIST_{ij}$	−0.00003	.
$POP_{ij,t}$	0.06205	
2006	−0.08194	*
2010	0.32739	***
2014	−0.14860	***
R^2	0.258	
$adj.R^2$	0.252	

Source Authors' own calculations
*** indicate a highly significant, ** very significant, * significant and . weakly significant coefficients

The two bilateral trade variables have, again, a significant positive effect on business cycle synchronization. Trade openness, however, has now a negative sign, but is not statistically significant. The time dummies indicate that there is one significant subperiod: the one that accounts for the financial crisis which has a positive impact on business cycle synchronization.[3] This is economically intuitive as the financial crisis was a symmetric common shock to all of them.

The estimation results for the full model (3.2) are given in Table 17.

Once again, the estimation of the full model (3.2) uncovers non-robust results and unsatisfactory significance. In Table 17 we observe similar inconsistencies for our estimates as we did for the estimates of the full period (model 3.1). The signs of deficit differentials and economic specialization become positive and bilateral trade volumes relative to GDP are associated to lower business cycle synchronization.

[3]The last subperiod, too, is significant in the regression with differentials in real effective exchange rates.

But there is no plausible reason that would make larger differences in fiscal policies and economic specialization yield more synchronized business cycles. Differences in fiscal deficits should be considered asymmetric shocks by themselves and economic specialization is expected to make countries more prone to idiosyncratic shocks. In a nutshell, these results are not only problematic with respect to statistical robustness but also with respect to economic intuition.

Moreover, we can observe a decrease in statistical significance for the independent variables in the full model (3.2) relative to the results of the simple regressions. This may be evidence for some sort of variance inflation linked to multicollinearity among explanatory variables. Thus, we continue with a VIF analysis, emphasizing the link of trade variables between themselves and with geographical distance, of exchange rate volatility with real interest rate volatility and of trade specialization with distances of fiscal deficits. Table 18 shows the results for the VIF analysis, which basically mirrors the steps taken for the entire period.

Once again, the use of trade specialization alongside deficit differentials as independent variables deliver very high *VIFs* (*VIFs* > 100). Thus, we remove trade specialization in the first step but still identify high *VIFs* for the two bilateral trade variables. Continuing without bilateral trade volumes as a fraction of GDP leaves us with interest rate differentials and exchange rate volatility as doubtful variables based on the interest rate parity hypothesis. Without differences in interest rates, estimation results show low *VIFs*. In order to make the results comparable to those of the regressions for the entire period we, again, remove geographical distance in the last column. Thus, we will follow the same rules in the selection of variables to estimate our subperiod models as we did for selecting those of the entire period regressions (see Table 13). In addition, we include dummy variables for the subperiods in order to control for the effects of the different phases of the EA.

As earlier, we would also like to measure the effect of EA membership on correlations. Given the problem of possible "channel variables" through which EA influences synchronization, we estimate Model M without them. In this case, correlations are regressed only on the gravity variables geographical distance, population and on the interactions of EA membership with the four subperiods. Estimation results are shown in Tables 19 and 20.

For eight variables the estimation results are striking. They are qualitatively the same as we found for the entire period. The coefficients of the

Table 18 VIF analysis for model (3.2)

Model	*Full model (3.2)*		*w/o* $TSI_{ij,t}$		*w/o* $BTY_{ij,t}$		*w/o* $RDIFF_{ij,t}$		*w/o* $DIST_{ij,t}$
Variable	*Coefficient (Standard error)*	*VIF*	*Coefficient (Standard error)*	*VIF*	*Coefficient (Standard error)*	*VIF*	*Coefficient (Standard error)*	*VIFs*	*Coefficient (Standard error)*
$KSI_{ij,t}$	0.00725 (0.03896)	1.05	−0.00398 (0.03896)	1.04	−0.00394 (0.03895)	1.04	0.00572 (0.04030)	1.04	0.01274 (0.03727)
$TSI_{ij,t}$	−0.10747 (0.03131)***	120.82							
$RDIFF_{ij,t}$	−0.01548 (0.00402)***	2.63	−0.01606 (0.00410)	2.62	−0.01606 (0.00409)***	2.62			
$DEFDIFF_{ij,t}$	0.09909 (0.03244)**	120.94	−0.01171 (0.00253)***	1.07	−0.01172 (0.00252)***	1.07	−0.01084 (0.00249)***	1.06	−0.01127 (0.002493)***
$BTT_{ij,t}$	1.56240 (1.08920)	7.24	1.5797 (1.11800)	7.24	1.47540 (0.60176)*	1.40	1.57200 (0.60145)**	1.40	2.43056 (0.51571)***
$BTY_{ij,t}$	−0.35022 (1.33530)	6.92	−0.14820 (1.34380)	6.91					
$TTY_{ij,t}$	−0.04620 (0.06302)	1.62	−0.06271 (0.06279)	1.60	−0.06468 (0.05578)	1.26	−0.07178 (0.05647)	1.26	−0.03090 (0.04845)
$ER\_Vol_{ij,t}$	−0.54463 (0.38620)	2.74	−0.53796 (0.39511)***	2.74	−0.05378 (0.39501)	2.74	−1.77510 (0.20464)***	1.10	−1.66254 (0.209881)***
$REFF\_ER_{ij,t}$	−0.01136 (0.00185)***	1.14	−0.01150 (0.00186)***	1.14	−0.01150 (0.00186)***	1.14	−0.01097 (0.00189)***	1.14	−0.01020 (0.00178)***
$DIST_{ij}$	−0.00003 (0.00002).	1.47	−0.00004 (0.00002)*	1.45	−0.00004 (0.00002)*	1.45	−0.00004 (0.00002)*	1.43	
$POP_{ij,t}$	0.06205 (0.04606)	1.20	0.02848 (0.04569)	1.13	0.02816 (0.04584)	1.12	0.03548 (0.04718)	1.12	0.05921 (0.0432588)

(continued)

Table 18 (continued)

Model	*Full model (3.2)*		*w/o* $TSI_{ij,t}$		*w/o* $BTY_{ij,t}$		*w/o* $RDIFF_{ij,t}$		*w/o* $DIST_{ij,t}$
Variable	*Coefficient (Standard error)*	*VIF*	*Coefficient (Standard error)*	*VIF*	*Coefficient (Standard error)*	*VIF*	*Coefficient (Standard error)*	*VIFs*	*Coefficient (Standard error)*
2006	−0.08194 (0.03324)*		−0.08459 (0.03344)*		−0.08465 (0.03345)*		−0.07483 (0.03242)*		−0.07110 (0.03073)*
2010	0.32739 (0.03484)***		0.33131 (0.03531)***		0.33121 (0.03534)***		0.36504 (0.03025)***		0.37008 (0.02776)***
2014	−0.14860 (0.03655)***		−0.15051 (0.03635)***		−0.15067 (0.03632)***		−0.13234 (0.03524)***		−0.12770 (0.03480)***
R^2	0.258		0.252		0.252		0.245		
$adj.R^2$	0.252		0.246		0.247		0.240		

Source Authors' own calculations

*** indicate a highly significant, ** very significant, * significant and . weakly significant coefficients

Table 19 Estimation results multiple regressions models A–H for subperiods

Variable/Model	*A*	*B*	*C*	*D*	*E*	*F*	*G*	*H*
$KSI_{ij,t}$								
$TSI_{ij,t}$					−0.01143	−0.01282	−0.01244	−0.01365
					(0.00233)***	(0.00234)***	(0.00231)***	(0.00232)***
$RDIFF_{ij,t}$			−0.02003	−0.02038			−0.02000)	−0.02034
			(0.00227)***	(0.00224)***			(0.00226)***	(0.00223)***
$DEFDIFF_{ij,t}$	0.01077	−0.01181	−0.01188	−0.01316				
	(0.00240)***	(0.00244)***	(0.00239)***	(0.00242)***				
$BTT_{ij,t}$	2.46504		2.22881		2.41285		2.17519	
	(0.50378)***		(0.49816)***		(0.50310)***		(0.49737)***	
$BTY_{ij,t}$		2.85518		2.53212		2.69619		2.45601
		(0.76551)***		(0.72228)***		(0.74168)***		(0.71860)***
$TTY_{ij,t}$		−0.07503		−0.07450		−0.08476		−0.07534
		(0.04761)		(0.04550)		(0.04650).		(0.04539).
$ER\_Vol_{ij,t}$	−1.65213	−1.66742			−1.64714	−1.66117		
	(0.20789)***	(0.20637)***			(0.20735)***	(0.20651)***		
$REFF\_ER_{ij,t}$	−0.01006	−0.01024	−0.01101	−0.01117	−0.01006	−0.01025	−0.01101	−0.01118
	(0.00178)***	(0.00180)***	(0.00167)***	(0.00170)***	(0.00178)***	(0.00182)***	(0.00166)***	(0.00170)***
$DIST_{ij}$								
$POP_{ij,t}$	0.06452	0.04629	0.05247		0.06624		0.05454	
	(0.04154)	(0.04283)	(0.04015)		(0.04141)		(0.04001)	
2006	−0.07102	−0.07121	−0.08101	−0.08143	−0.07070	−0.07033	−0.08070	−0.08101
	(0.03061)*	(0.03075)*	(0.03153)*	(0.03174)*	(0.03059)*	(0.03082)*	(0.03152)*	(0.03172)*
2010	0.36965	0.37024	0.32632	0.32693	0.37021	0.37202	0.32683	0.32749
	(0.02724)***	(0.02770)***	(0.02948)***	(0.02989)***	(0.02725)***	(0.02776)***	(0.02950)***	(0.02990)***
2014	−0.12960	−0.12844	−0.15114	−0.14962	−0.12918	−0.12603	−0.15074	−0.14887
	(0.03335)***	(0.03408)***	(0.03516)***	(0.03577)***	(0.03336)***	(0.03411)***	(0.03517)***	(0.03581)***
R^2	0.240	0.238	0.248	0.246	0.241	0.239	0.250	0.248
$adj.R^2$	0.236	0.234	0.245	0.243	0.237	0.235	0.246	0.244
AIC	−2676.1	−2670.6	−2694.3	−2690.5	−2679.0	−2673.7	−2697.4	−2693.6

Source Authors' own calculations

In the first line the estimated coefficients are given, in the second the standard errors. *** indicate a highly significant, ** very significant, * significant and . weakly significant coefficients

Table 20 Models I–M for the subperiod analysis

Variable/Model	*I*	*J*	*K*	*L*	*M*
KSI_{ij}	−0.00704	−0.02135	−0.00578	−0.01990	
	(0.04140)	(0.03885)	(0.04127)	(0.03874)	
TSI_{ij}			−0.01129	−0.01246	
			(0.00231)***	(0.00228)***	
$RDIFF_{ij}$		−0.02104		−0.02100	
		(0.00219)***		(0.00219)***	
$DEFDIFF_{ij}$	−0.01061	−0.01188			
	(0.00240)***	(0.00238)***			
BTT_{ij}					
BTY_{ij}					
TTY_{ij}					
ER_Vol_{ij}	−1.81920		−1.81150		
	(0.20427)***		(0.20383)***		
$REFF\_ER_{ij}$	−0.01094	−0.01186	−0.01092	−0.01183	
	(0.00193)***	(0.00180)***	(0.00193)***	(0.00180)***	
$DIST_{ij}$	−0.00005	−0.00004	−0.00005	−0.00004	−0.00005
	(0.00001)***	(0.00001)***	(0.00001)***	(0.00001)***	(0.00001)***
POP_{ij}					−0.01018
					(0.04754)
2006	−0.07710	−0.08449	−0.07669	−0.08415	0.01594
	(0.03243)*	(0.03441)*	(0.03240)*	(0.03435)*	(0.03242)
2010	0.36204	0.31923	0.36274	0.31988	0.48050
	(0.03023)***	(0.03317)***	(0.03023)***	(0.03315)***	(0.02946)***
2014	−0.14208	−0.15981	−0.14149	−0.15926	0.04223
	(0.03475)***	(0.03589)***	(0.03480)**	(0.03593)***	(0.02941)

(continued)

Table 20 (continued)

Variable/Model	*I*	*J*	*K*	*L*	*M*
EA ∗ 2002					0.70896
					(0.09210)***
EA ∗ 2006					−0.61716
					(0.09429)***
EA ∗ 2010					0.18790
					(0.07069)**
EA ∗ 2014					0.05929
					(0.05642)
R^2	0.237	0.245	0.239	0.247	0.228
$adj.R^2$	0.233	0.242	0.235	0.243	0.224
AIC	−2671.2	−2688.3	−2673.9	−2691.3	

Source Authors' own calculations

In the first line the estimated coefficients are given, in the second the standard errors. *** indicate a highly significant, ** very significant, * significant and . weakly significant coefficients

two specialization variables, the two economic policy variables, the two bilateral trade variables, exchange rate volatility and geographical distance did not change signs. Thus, trade specialization is negatively related to business cycle synchronization, as well as distances in economic policies and in geography. Bilateral trade increases synchronization whereas the volatility of nominal exchange rates has a negative effect.

For three variables, i.e., trade openness, competitiveness distance, and population gravity there are differences compared to the analysis of the entire period:

- Trade openness is not related positively anymore to synchronization, although one expected a positive relationship. Even in the simple regression the sign of the regression coefficient associated to this variable is negative. However, statistical significance is limited as it only is present in two model specifications.
- The competitiveness variable, i.e., distance in real effective exchange rates, is significant in all models now. As before, the relationship of this variable with synchronization is negative. This means that distances in competitiveness lowers synchronization. But why do we find overall significance in the subperiod setting for this coefficient? We suppose that the shorter periods do not allow price adjustments due to rigidity. This makes distances likelier. Thus, broader distances in real effective exchange rates in the short run can better explain synchronization in comparison to the more restricted distances in the long run.
- The population gravity is not significant any longer.

The time dummies are significant in all models except for two of them in model M. Compared to the base subperiod (1999–2002) synchronization is lower in the run-up to the financial crisis and during the sovereign debt crisis of the last subperiod (2011–2014). Likely, the lower synchronization from 2002 to 2006 is associated to a diverging level of economic development in the periphery and the core. From 2011 to 2014, the sovereign debt crisis hindered economic recovery in those countries that were hit hardest by the financial crisis. The period ranging from 2007 to 2010, however, contains the symmetric shock of the financial crisis that drove business cycles in the EA. The coefficient associated to this period dummy is positive and significant indicating higher economic synchronization among EA countries.

In regression M, we can notice that from 2007 to 2010 the coefficient associated to the time dummy increases. Likely, this is linked to both the financial crisis of 2007 and the sovereign debt crisis from 2010. When looking at the interaction variables, we can notice that EA countries experienced a lower correlation in the prior period to the crisis (2003–2006) compared to other countries. This negative effect converts into a significant positive effect during the crisis subperiod (2007–2010). This shows us that in the extreme situation of the financial crisis, a unified central bank was not a negative characteristic of the Euro in the general perspective as it is frequently argued. This argument, however, could be disputed. One could argue that the ECB could pave the road to growth below potential for all members so that they would be "synchronized in poverty." A higher economic correlation between Euro members is also verified for the first period from 1998 to 2002.

3.3 *Estimations for the Sample Including Financial Integration*

Until here, we ignored financial integration in the analysis. Now it is time to consider cross-border capital stocks, i.e., assets and liabilities of a country in another country, as proxy for financial integration. We would expect that the higher the average of assets and liabilities of one country from another, the deeper their financial integration.

Due to lack of data availability we have to restrict our analysis to the following countries: Austria, Belgium, Finland, France, Germany, Greece, Ireland, Italy, Luxembourg, Netherlands, Spain, Denmark, Sweden, UK, and Switzerland. The averages of cross-border capital stocks are calculated for the time period ranging from mid-2007 to the end of 2014.

Thus, our full model in this case is given by Eq. (3):

$$\begin{aligned} COR_{ij} = {} & \beta_0 + \beta_1 KSI_{ij} + \beta_2 TSI_{ij} + \beta_3 RDIFF_{ij} + \beta_4 DEFDIFF_{ij} + \beta_5 BTT_{ij} + \beta_6 BTY_{ij} + \beta_7 TTY_{ij} \\ & + \beta_8 ER\_Vol_{ij} + \beta_9 REFF\_ER_{ij} + \beta_{10} DIST_{ij} + \beta_{11} POP_{ij} + \beta_{12} CAP\_Stocks_{ij} + \varepsilon_{ij} \end{aligned} \tag{3}$$

Before we run our multiple regression models, we follow the same procedure used in the last sections, which start with the estimations of simple regressions (Table 21).

All coefficients seem to have the correct sign in this case, even though we do not observe statistical significance for the following variables: population difference, volatility of the nominal exchange rate, and trade

Table 21 Estimation results for simple regression models including financial integration

Independent variable	*Coefficient*	*Significance level*	R^2
KSI_{ij}	−2.68624	***	0.37
TSI_{ij}	−0.09496	***	0.50
$RDIFF_{ij}$	−0.44050	***	0.65
$DEFDIFF_{ij}$	−0.09570	***	0.46
BTT_{ij}	2.60103	***	0.11
BTY_{ij}	3.00441	*	0.08
TTY_{ij}	0.09330		0.00
ER_Vol_{ij}	−0.02305		0.16
$REFF\_ER_{ij}$	−0.00984	*	0.04
$DIST_{ij}$	−0.00013	***	0.22
POP_{ij}	0.10032		0.01
CAP_Stocks_{ij}	0.03071		0.01

Source Authors' own calculations
*** indicate a highly significant, ** very significant, * significant and . weakly significant coefficients

openness. Furthermore, our key variable of this section, i.e., financial integration measured by cross-border capital stocks, is not statistically significant.

We go on with the estimation of the full model given by Eq. (3), whose results are presented in Table 22.

Like the results for estimations of Eq. (1), the coefficients of Eq. (3) can be seen as unsatisfactory as many of their signs change compared to their respective estimations in the simple regression setting. This is the case for the coefficients related to economic specialization, deficit differentials, bilateral trade intensity measured with respect to the GDP, nominal exchange rate volatility and geographical distance. The signs of these coefficients, if robust, would challenge economic reasoning. In this case however, results are not robust because the signs change when compared to results obtained with simple regressions. Once again, this could be seen as a symptom of multicollinearity. Thus, in order to go on with our analysis, we follow the standard *VIF* analysis conducted in earlier sections. Table 23 offers the results for the *VIF* analysis. If we remove the differentials of fiscal deficits or the distances in real effective exchange rates instead of the difference in real interest rates, we get the following results as shown in Table 24.

Table 22 Estimation results for the full model (3.3)

Variable/Model	*Model 3.3 (coefficients)*
KSI_{ij}	0.27170
TSI_{ij}	−0.16085*
$RDIFF_{ij}$	−0.50038***
$DEFDIFF_{ij}$	0.14979*
BTT_{ij}	0.71023
BTY_{ij}	−0.83265
TTY_{ij}	0.04586
ER_Vol_{ij}	4.99900***
$REFF\_ER_{ij}$	−0.02289**
$DIST_{ij}$	0.00001
POP_{ij}	0.05588.
CAP_Stocks_{ij}	0.00730
R^2	0.939
$adj.R^2$	0.928

Source Authors' own calculations

*** indicate a highly significant, ** very significant, * significant and . weakly significant coefficients

Once again, the complete model delivers two extremely high *VIFs* (*VIFs* > 100) for the variables trade specialization and deficit differentials. So, we follow with the estimations of column 2 where we remove trade specialization. In this case, we can observe again high *VIFs* for the variables *BTT* and *BTY*. Thus, *BTY* is removed from the model and we follow with estimations of column 3.

Here we observe a difference compared to the earlier framework: both differentials in interest rates and deficits are high and comparable. Thus, we remove the former variable in column 4 as we did in the earlier sections. This still delivers high *VIFs* for the variables volatility and distances in real effective exchange rates. Thus, we could go on by removing the difference in real effective exchange rates or the one in volatilities. If we remove the difference in real effective exchange rates, we arrive in the estimations of column 5. Given an inverted sign in *BTT* and to follow the standard of prior regressions, we decided to follow our earlier decision to remove the variable distance in column 6, even though the sign of the coefficient related to this variable continues to be negative.

Table 24 offers the results for the final columns should we have instead removed the difference in real exchange rates in column 4 of Table 23 instead of differences in interest rates and then followed with

Table 23 VIF analysis for model (3.3) including financial integration

Model	*Full model (3.3)*		*w/o* TSI_{ij}		*w/o* BTY_{ij}		*w/o* $RDIFF_{ij}$		*w/o* $REFF\_ER_{ij}$		*w/o* $DIST_{ij}$	
Variable	*Coefficient (Standard error)*	*VIF*	*Coefficient (Standard error)*	*VIF*	*Coefficient (Standard error)*	*VIF*	*Coefficient (Standard error)*	*VIF*	*Coefficient (Standard error)*	*VIF*	*Coefficient (Standard error)*	*VIF*
KSI_{ij}	0.27170 (0.24918)	2.50	0.24489 (0.24485)	2.49	0.27116 (0.23882)	2.46	−0.78058 (0.44803).	2.29	−1.36070 (0.42434)**	1.92	−1.35389 (0.38839)***	1.77
TSI_{ij}	−0.16085 (0.06497)*	232.8										
$RDIFF_{ij}$	−0.50038 (0.03259)***	3.75	−0.53910 (0.03313)***	2.94	−0.54109 (0.03357)***	2.93						
$DEFDIFF_{ij}$	0.14979 (0.06822)*	212.4	−0.01191 (0.00931)	3.15	−0.01276 (0.00913)	3.12	−0.05877 (0.01749)**	2.80	−0.07001 (0.01577)***	2.67	−0.06983 (0.01366)***	2.57
BTT_{ij}	0.71023 (0.67529)	11.2	0.91219 (0.69113)	11.1	0.12708 (0.34115)	2.28	−0.08190 (0.74987)	2.28	−0.16253 (0.81860)	2.28	−0.18302 (0.64551)	1.86
BTY_{ij}	−0.83265 (0.54644)	8.87	−1.02860 (0.61494).	8.81								
TTY_{ij}	0.04586 (0.04829)	3.09	0.05057 (0.04500)	3.08	0.00863 (0.03384)	1.65	0.02348 (0.09614)	1.65	0.01874 (0.10258)	1.65	0.01674 (0.08679)	1.43
ER_Vol_{ij}	4.99900 (0.65204)***	19.3	5.99570 (0.69024)***	14.3	5.99080 (0.69713)***	14.3	3.86600 (1.67940)*	13.9	−0.34015 (0.70640)	1.81	−0.34432 (0.63062)	1.77
$REFF\_ER_{ij}$	−0.02289 (0.00598)**	17.8	−0.02964 (0.00659)***	14.7	−0.02975 (0.00664)***	14.7	−0.03944 (0.01583)*	14.6				
$DIST_{ij}$	0.00001 (0.00001)	2.78	0.00002 (0.00001).	2.61	0.00002 (0.00001)	2.58	−0.00000 (0.00004)	2.55	0.00000 (0.00004)	2.55		
POP_{ij}	0.05588 (0.02941).	1.54	0.04676 (0.02925)	1.52	0.03458 (0.02676)	1.36	0.16283 (0.07429)*	1.30	0.17307 (0.08086)*	1.30	0.17186 (0.06788)*	1.19
CAP_Stocks_{ij}	0.00730 (0.00914)	1.98	0.01173 (0.00937)	1.91	0.01343 (0.00971)	1.86	0.026443 (0.01874)	1.85	0.01750 (0.02023)	1.81	0.01733 (0.01861)	1.78
R^2	0.939		0.933		0.932		0.596		0.550		0.550	
$adj.R^2$	0.928		0.922		0.922		0.542		0.498		0.505	

Source Authors' own calculations

*** indicate a highly significant, ** very significant, * significant and . weakly significant coefficients

Table 24 VIF analysis for the removement of one distance measure: real interest rates, real effective exchange rates, or fiscal deficits

Model	*w/o* $REFF\_ER_{ij}$		*w/o* $DEFDIFF_{ij}$	
Variable	*Coefficient (Standard error)*	*VIF*	*Coefficient (Standard error)*	*VIF*
KSI_{ij}	−0.13635 (0.28208)	2.13	0.17783 (0.21283)	2.29
TSI_{ij}				
$RDIFF_{ij}$	−0.55474 (0.04267)***	2.91	−0.55630 (0.02960)***	2.63
$DEFDIFF_{ij}$	−0.02001 (0.00971)*	3.02		
BTT_{ij}	0.07203 (0.39741)	2.28	0.35896 (0.26127)	1.94
BTY_{ij}				
TTY_{ij}	0.00470 (0.03680)	1.65	0.01520 (0.03465)	1.64
ER_Vol_{ij}	2.89760 (0.51960)***	2.74	6.29130 (0.65896)***	13.28
$REFF\_ER_{ij}$			−0.03146 (0.00658)***	14.25
$DIST_{ij}$	0.00003 (0.00002)	2.57	0.00001 (0.00001)	2.51
POP_{ij}	0.03900 (0.03495)	1.36	0.03342 (0.02848)	1.36
CAP_Stocks_{ij}	0.00641 (0.00967)	1.82	0.01277 (0.00925)	1.86
R^2	0.906		0.930	
$adj.R^2$	0.894		0.920	

Source Authors' own calculations

*** indicate a highly significant, ** very significant, * significant and . weakly significant coefficients

removing deficit differentials. Observe that when using two of the variables differences in real exchange rates, deficit differentials, and interest rate differentials together, estimations continue to deliver *VIFs* that are uncomfortably high (close to 3). Thus, we decided only to use each of these variables individually in our estimations.

In summary, for this restricted period of data and country selection our estimations that include capital stocks will account for the following rules, where we do not:

- Use trade specialization together with deficit differentials;
- Use *BTT* and *BTY* in a single model;
- Use the trade variables *BTT*, *BTY*, and *TTY* together with geographical distance in order to follow the same standard as in prior estimations;
- Use exchange rate volatility together with real exchange rate differentials;
- Use more than one of the following differential variables in a model: real exchange rate, interest rate, and deficit.

With these different restrictions and including the variable capital stocks, we achieve the following model settings given by Table 25.

Estimation results for the different models are given by Tables 26 and 27. Notice that in order to organize results and to save space, models of Table 25 that deliver the same selected independent variables according to the *AIC* criterion are written together in the same column. We would also like to check whether capital stocks increase synchronization within the EA. Thus, we estimate models M1 and M2 where "channel variables" are not considered. In these models, synchronization is explained by capital stocks, by the two gravity variables and by the interaction term between capital stocks and EA.

The main findings are:

Specialization and Policy Variables
When we include financial integration, all specialization and policy variables are significant and decrease synchronization. We can observe that economic specialization is now relevant in more models compared to our prior sections.

Trade Variables
Except for one case (Model C), we observe a negative effect of all three variables on synchronization, which can be seen as a paradox compared to our prior results. Moreover, when checking for robustness of these estimates, we notice that the sign of these coefficients invert in relation to the simple regression results. Thus, we should be careful when interpreting these results.

Exchange Rates
The nominal exchange volatility is not any longer relevant since it is not selected as independent variable in any of the models by the *AIC*

Table 25 Multiple regression models including financial integration

Variable/Model	*A1*	*A2*	*A3*	*B1*	*B2*	*B3*	*C*	*D*	*E1*	*E2*	*F1*	*F2*	*G1*	*G2*	*H1*	*H2*	*I1*	*I2*	*I3*	*J1*	*J2*	*K1*	*K2*	*L1*	*L2*
CAP_STOCKS_{ij}	✓	✓	✓	✓	✓	✓	✓	✓	✓	✓	✓	✓	✓	✓	✓	✓	✓	✓	✓	✓	✓	✓	✓	✓	✓
KSI_{ij}	✓	✓	✓	✓	✓	✓	✓	✓	✓	✓	✓	✓	✓	✓	✓	✓	✓	✓	✓	✓	✓	✓	✓	✓	✓
TSI_{ij}									✓	✓	✓	✓	✓	✓	✓	✓						✓	✓	✓	✓
$RDIFF_{ij}$							✓	✓					✓		✓					✓				✓	
$DEFDIFF_{ij}$	✓	✓		✓	✓												✓	✓		✓	✓				
BTT_{ij}	✓	✓	✓				✓		✓	✓			✓	✓											
BTY_{ij}				✓	✓	✓		✓			✓	✓			✓	✓									
TTY_{ij}	✓	✓	✓	✓	✓	✓	✓	✓	✓	✓	✓	✓	✓	✓	✓	✓									
ER_Vol_{ij}	✓			✓					✓		✓						✓					✓			
$REFF\_ER_{ij}$			✓			✓				✓		✓		✓		✓			✓		✓		✓		✓
$DIST_{ij}$																	✓	✓	✓	✓	✓	✓	✓	✓	✓
POP_{ij}	✓	✓	✓	✓	✓	✓	✓	✓	✓	✓	✓	✓	✓	✓	✓	✓	✓	✓	✓	✓	✓	✓	✓	✓	✓

Source Authors' own calculations

Table 26 Estimation results for models A1-A3, B1-B3, C, D, E1-E2, F1-F2, G1-G2, H1-H2, K1-K2, L2, I1, I2, J1

Variable/Model	*A1=A2=B1=B2=I1=I2=J1*	*A3=B3*	*C*	*D*	*E1=F1=K1*	*E2=F2=K2=L2*	*G1*	*G2=H2*	*H1*
KSI_{ij}	−1.38491 (0.37428)***	−2.49850 (0.40676)***	−2.35052 (0.42818)***	−0.85109 (0.33978)*	−1.15598 (0.35184)**	−1.03646 (0.33876)**		−1.03646 (0.33876)**	
TSI_{ij}					−0.07354 (0.01090)***	−0.07126 (0.01083)***	−0.04933 (0.00945)***	−0.07126 (0.01083)***	−0.04687 (0.00891)***
$RDIFF_{ij}$				−0.42777 (0.04479)***			−0.38902 (0.03672)***		−0.38853 (0.03603)***
$DEFDIFF_{ij}$	-0.06829 (0.01108)***								
BTT_{ij}			1.37091 (0.56250)*				−0.99956 (0.39103)*		
BTY_{ij}									−1.12834 (0.45383)*
TTY_{ij}				−0.14091 (0.04384)**			−0.15132 (0.03747)***		−0.11119 (0.04084)**
ER_Vol_{ij}									
$REFF\_ER_{ij}$		−0.00952 (0.00528).	−0.00824 (0.00575)			−0.00700 (0.00515)		−0.00700 (0.00515)	
$DIST_{ij}$									
POP_{ij}	0.16674 (0.06872)*	0.16698 (0.07992)*	0.18379 (0.06951)*		0.16770 (0.06609)*	0.17106 (0.06559)*		0.17106 (0.06559)*	
CAP_Stocks_{ij}	0.00813 (0.01380)	0.05146 (0.02334)*	0.03474 (0.02165)	0.05663 (0.00905)***	0.00434 (0.01311)	0.02276 (0.01885)	0.04826 (0.00985)***	0.02276 (0.01885)	0.04522 (0.01026)***
$CAP\_Stocks_{ij} * EA$									
R^2	0.547		0.466	0.778	0.579	0.605	0.818	0.592	0.816
$adj.R^2$	0.522		0.429	0.766	0.556	0.572	0.805	0.564	0.803
AIC	−259.8	−243.5	−244.9	−315.4	−265.5	−266.0	−328.7	−266.0	−327.9

Source Authors' own calculations

In the first line the estimated coefficients are given, in the second the standard errors. *** indicate a highly significant, ** very significant, * significant and . weakly significant coefficients

Table 27 Estimation results for models I3, J2-J3, L1, M1-M2

Variable/Model	*I3=J3*	*J2*	*L1*	*M1*	*M2*
KSI_{ij}	−1.26180	−0.91940			
	(0.38952)**	(0.37003)*			
TSI_{ij}			−0.04299		
			(0.00822)***		
$RDIFF_{ij}$		−0.39953	−0.35820		
		(0.05034)***	(0.04422)***		
$DEFDIFF_{ij}$	−0.066599				
	(0.01541)***				
BTT_{ij}					
BTY_{ij}					
TTY_{ij}					
ER_Vol_{ij}					
$REFF\_ER_{ij}$	−0.00741				
	(0.00587)				
$DIST_{ij}$	0.00000			−0.00014	−0.00014
	(0.00003)			(0.00003)***	(0.00003)***
POP_{ij}	0.17095	0.08238		0.10391	0.08427
	(0.06644)*	(0.05057)		(0.10375)	(0.10474)
CAP_Stocks_{ij}	0.02809	0.05777	0.04159	−0.00458	−0.00766
	(0.02169)	(0.01014)***	(0.01134)***	(0.02487)	(0.02272)
$CAP\_Stocks_{ij} * EA$					0.07881
					(0.04191).
R^2	0.562	0.768	0.801	0.242	0.262
$adj.R^2$	0.525	0.756	0.790	0.211	0.221
AIC	−244.5	−312.2	−23.8		

Source Authors' own calculations

In the first line the estimated coefficients are given, in the second the standard errors. *** indicate a highly significant, ** very significant, * significant and . weakly significant coefficients

criterion. Likely, this is a consequence of the sample period used in this section (after 2007), when almost all countries selected are EA members and thus have fixed exchange rates by definition. On the other hand, real effective exchange rates are weakly significant but only in two models.

Gravity Variables

The two gravity variables geographical distance and population have opposite sings. Differently than in the prior estimations, population is statistically significant in almost all models. On the other hand, distance is only relevant to our estimations, when channel variables are neglected in models M1 and M2.

Financial Integration

The variable that proxies financial integration, capital stocks is often significant and has a positive sign. This indicates that capital stocks contribute to financial integration and consequently to synchronization. This significance is weak because it is lost when we do not control for the different independent variables in model M1. However, we can notice in Model M2 that the coefficient related to the interaction of capital stocks and EA membership is positive and weakly significant. Thus, we could state that more than for other countries the variable financial integration plays an important role in lifting business cycle synchronization in EA members.

References

Baxter, M., & King, R. G. (1999). Measuring Business Cycles: Approximate Band-Pass Filters for Economic Time Series. *Review of Economics and Statistics, 81*(4), 575–593.

Böwer, U., & Guillemineau, C. (2006). *Determinants of Business Cycle Synchronization across Euro Area Countries* (ECB Working Paper, 587).

Dreyer, J. K., & Schmid, P. A. (2015). Fiscal Federalism in Monetary unions: Hypothetical Fiscal Transfers Within the Euro-Zone. *International Review of Applied Economics, 29*(4), 506–532.

Woitek, U. (1998). *A Note on the Baxter-King Filter* (Working Paper). Business School—Economics, University of Glasgow.

CHAPTER 4

Discussion

Abstract This chapter concludes our pivot. It discusses the results of our empirical investigation considering the OCA literature. Moreover, the chapter offers reflections upon policies that could be adopted to foster more synchronization of business cycles in the EA. The chapter moves from an initial general discussion into the reflection on what can be learnt from the relationship of each independent variable with the level of business cycle correlation.

Keywords Concluding remarks · Discussion of results · Policy recommendations · Learning outcomes · Fostering synchronization

In this chapter we conclude our work. Section 1 summarizes the discussion of this pivot and reflects upon the implications of our empirical results for the EA. Based thereon, Sect. 2 draws policy recommendations on what could be done to foster business cycles synchronization among EA countries.

1 Status Quo

Low business cycle synchronization across regions complicates stabilization policies in currency unions. As the EA consists of different countries, the academic literature and the general public often ascribe structural

J. Kabderian Dreyer and P. A. Schmid,
Optimal Currency Areas and the Euro, Volume I,
https://doi.org/10.1007/978-3-030-46515-5_4

economic problems to the Euro. Thus, the common currency becomes an easy scapegoat for political allegations.

The Eurosceptics have strong arguments against the Euro like the risk of moral hazard and the political risk of disintegration of the common market. In this debate, it is relevant to ask to what extent the criteria for an optimum currency area are fulfilled in the EA and whether—in line with the endogeneity view—the scope of the shortcomings has become smaller since the Euro's introduction.

The gold standard in the literature is a comparison of the European countries with regions in the United States. Our analysis compared the correlation coefficients among EU and EA countries with the ones among US states. The results are straightforward: for all periods considered the EA member countries show a much higher level of correlation of GDPs than their US counterparts, irrespective of filtering the GDP time series for trends. The highest levels of correlation are observed for the original 11 EA member countries. It is true, however, that the level of correlation dropped severely in the aftermath of the sovereign debt crisis in the EA. Whereas correlation coefficients decreased in the United States, too, the standard deviation of the coefficients was slightly higher in the EA from the last quarter of 2011 to the third quarter of 2015 in comparison to the United States; the variation coefficient, though, is smaller in the EA. On average EA countries still enjoy more cyclical correlation. The difference is remarkable for the original 11 members whose standard deviation is still clearly smaller than in the United States. In a nutshell: the level of synchronization is higher in the EA than in the United States. Even though there has been less synchronization in the last four years until 2015q3, this development is also observable for the United States.

The evolution of synchronization is remarkable, too. Going back to the 1960s and analyzing three subperiods (from 1963q1, 1998q1, and 2003q1 until 2015q3) clearly shows increased synchronization over time. The original 11 EA members have an overall average cyclical correlation coefficient of 0.6357 but 0.8194 for the third subperiod. During the same time, the standard deviation declined making the variation coefficient even smaller. Globally, business cycles became more synchronized, too, as the benchmark groups for all three time periods show. EA countries not only became more synchronized among themselves but globally as well. Consequently, one has to distinguish two stylized facts. First, the European integration is related to higher levels of business cycle synchronization. Second, this process is overlapped by the emergence of a global business cycle. It is clear, however, that synchronization attained higher levels in the EA than in the United States and globally. Consequently, the argument of low levels of business cycle synchronization is a powerful narrative but is, in fact, not observed in the EA.

There is a set of independent variables that is associated with business cycle synchronization. We distinguished specialization variables, policy variables, trade variables, exchange rates, and gravity variables. In addition, we considered dummies for EA membership and interactions. The relationships between these variables and synchronization were analyzed for the entire period ranging from 1999 to 2014, for four subperiods between 1999 and 2014 and for a shorter period from mid-2007 to 2014. In addition, this last period considers financial integration as explaining variable. Results for the cross-sectional and panel regressions are summarized in Table 1, where the signs for the regression coefficients are given. In case there is no overall clear tendency or there is no significance a question mark is used instead of a sign.

The evidence for trade variables is mixed. There are more arguments for larger trade volumes to favor synchronization supporting the view that intra-industry trade plays a larger role than inter-industry trade.

Financial integration is associated to increased synchronization. When controlled for an interaction term between EA and capital stocks, we find out that the coefficient related to capital stocks alone is positive and statistically significant in many models. Moreover, when removing "all channel variables"—through which EA could affect synchronization—the interaction coefficient between EA and capital stocks is weakly significant. Thus, we conclude that financial integration especially influences synchronization in the case of EA members.

When ignoring possible channel variables, the coefficient related to the dummy EA is statistically significant and indicates that belonging to the EA increases correlations.

Concerning the analysis with subperiods, we can observe that relative to the base period (1999–2002) only the period of the financial crisis is associated to higher business cycle synchronization. However, when looking at this effect for EA members only the period preceding the crisis is related to less synchronization. Most importantly, we can observe that especially during the financial crisis, the cyclical GDP components of EA members presented an even higher correlation, which is intuitive due to the common shock of the financial crisis.

Table 1 Overview of signs of regression coefficients

Variable	*Total sample 1999–2014* Entire period	*Total sample 1999–2014* Subperiods	*Restricted sample mid-2007–2014* Including financial integration
KSI_{ij}	?	?	–
TSI_{ij}	–	–	–
$RDIFF_{ij}$	–	–	–
$DEFDIFF_{ij}$	–	–	–
BTT_{ij}	+	+	?
BTY_{ij}	+	+	–/?
TTY_{ij}	+	–/?	–
ER_Vol_{ij}	–	–	?
$REFF\_ER_{ij}$	–/?	–	–/?
$DIST_{ij}$	–	–	–/?
POP_{ij}	+	?	+
CAP_Stocks_{ij}			+/?
2006		–	
2010		+	
2014		–	
EA	+		
EA ∗ 2002		+	
EA ∗ 2006		–	
EA ∗ 2010		+	
EA ∗ 2014		?	
$CAP\_Stocks_{ij} * EA$			+

Source Authors' own calculations
+ for positive relationships; – for negative; and ? for nonsignificant and/or no clear relationships

2 Prospects for Economic Policies

2.1 *Real Interest Rates*

Interest rate spreads have been historically low during the Euro's entire history. They narrowed along the path from the Maastricht Treaty to the Euro's introduction in 1999. In all four subperiods from 1999 to 2014 the median distance was below 2% and decreased (see Fig. 1). The introduction of the common currency reduced perceived country-specific risk, as exchange rate risk vanished and capital markets assumed that an exit from the EA would be impossible. The interquartile range that gives the interval for 50% of the distances is relatively low. It only

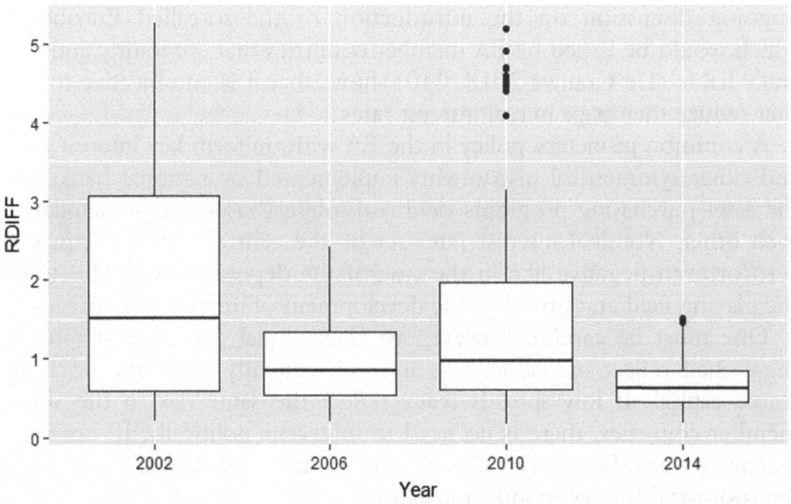

Fig. 1 Differences in real interest rates over time (*Source* Authors)

increased in the aftermath of the financial crisis when people realized that country-specific risk still existed. However, after the implementation of rescue packages and no observation of exits from the EA, the spreads' variation returned to its previous low levels.

In the meantime, the EA developed the European Stability Mechanism (ESM), an intergovernmental agency that applies financial instruments like sovereign bailout loans to secure financial stability among its members. Recipient countries are evaluated and must usually comply with requirements like structural economic reforms in order to receive funds. As of today, the ESM and its forerunner EFSF, for example, holds just over 55% of the Greek public debt[1]. Given this mechanism it is expected that increasing real interest rate spreads are an unlikely event in the EA. The close relation of interest rates is due to the high credibility of Northern and central EA member countries. Policymakers discuss further instruments that aim at preserving low spreads and even closing the small remaining gaps between real interest rates. The

[1] An overview over the financial assistance granted by the ESM and the EFSF to Greece is available at https://www.esm.europa.eu/assistance/greece/explainer-esm-and-efsf-financial-assistance-greece (last access February 17, 2020).

ongoing discussion on the introduction of the so-called Eurobonds which would be issued by EA member countries that are jointly and severally liable (De Grauwe 2018, 240) shows that it is an objective to further reduce their gaps in real interest rates.

A common monetary policy in the EA with uniform key interest rates and other symmetrical instruments implemented by national banks like the asset purchasing programs yield real interest rates that are similar to each other. Nominal interest rates set by the central bank are equal to zero or even negative like in the case of the deposit facility. This levels the playing field and prohibits the development of interest rate spreads.

One must be careful, however, to chase equal real interest rates as these shall reflect individual risk and consequently show the price for scarce capital. If low spreads really reflect the same risk in the single member countries, there is no need to intervene politically. If, however, policies cover different risk classes, misallocations of capital could build the root for future economic imbalances.

2.2 *Fiscal Deficits*

With a uniform monetary policy, fiscal policy is usually considered more important for stabilization of business cycles. This would make differences in national fiscal policies necessary to counteract idiosyncratic economic shocks. On the other hand, fiscal policy by itself can be seen as an economic shock to business cycles whose direction of impact might be measured by fiscal deficits. Thus, low distances in deficits would mean similar fiscal policies fostering similar business cycles. National governments, therefore, should make sure that differentials in fiscal deficits are not too high. The development in the EA shows that median differences are below 5%, thus generally not large. In the aftermath of the financial crisis differentials and their variations increased (Fig. 2).

In this light, the Euro's parents agreed in the Maastricht treaty on convergence criteria that limited national fiscal deficits to 3% and overall government debt to 60% of the GDP (De Grauwe 2018, 227–228). These provisions later were concretized and are called Stability and Growth Pact today. Given an inflation target of 2% and a real growth rate of 1%, fiscal deficits of 3% would keep relative public debt constant (De Grauwe 2018, 223). Beyond this common rule there was an agreement for coordination and that the EU's budget shall support beta convergence.

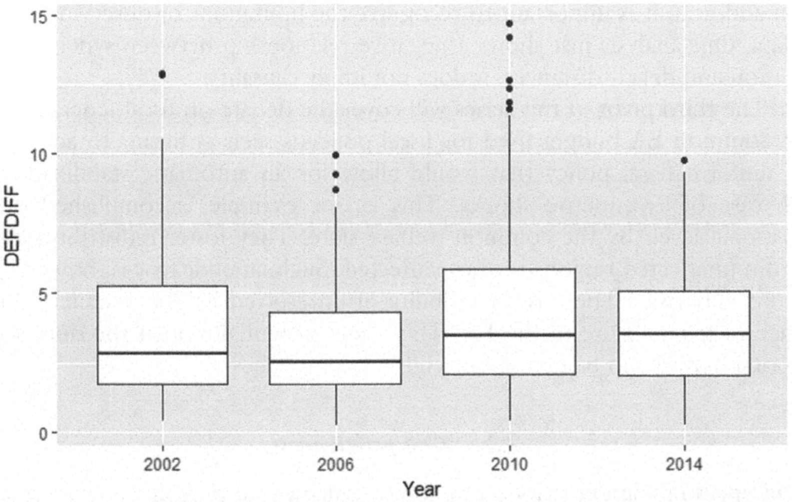

Fig. 2 Differences in deficits as percentage of GDP over time (*Source* Authors)

As the limits have been considered too restrictive and some member countries including Germany and France infringed the common rules, there were amendments in the mid-2000s that allowed accounting for individual circumstances. The rules for sovereign debt were strengthened again in the early 2010s, especially those for sanctions. These are commonly seen as severe limits to national fiscal policies that are hindered to stabilize national economies (De Grauwe 2018, 238). Nevertheless, one can interpret the development of new fiscal monitoring tools as a step toward fiscal policy and thus toward fiscal deficit convergence. It is important to monitor the evolvement of individual deficits and make sure that countries comply with the rules approved. On the other hand, one could argue that surpluses must be regulated, too, in order to limit deficit differentials. This is not the case today, but policymakers should be aware that differences coming from surpluses might be a sign for divergent business cycles.

Generally, policies to reduce differences in deficits shall be applied with caution as the need for different fiscal policies might just be the result of asymmetric shocks that affect national business cycles. Thus, one should allow distances in fiscal deficits for stabilization purposes.

In addition, it is important to recognize the limitations of observing our data. Our analysis just shows a negative relationship between synchronization and deficit distances, it does not imply causality.

The third pivot of this series will cover the debate on fiscal federalism. A common EA budget used for fiscal policy is seen as means to achieve a uniform fiscal policy that would allow for an automatic stabilization in case of asymmetric shocks. This is, for example, accomplished on national levels by the common welfare state. They foster redistributions from unaffected regions to those affected. Such an endeavor is, however, politically risky. There is a possibility of unresolved liability parallel to a lack of federal state in the EA. This could potentially open the door to moral hazard and beggar-your-neighbor approaches.

2.3 *Competitiveness*

Distances in competitivity are an important root for prolonged economic imbalances. This is even more important in currency unions, which by definition do not allow for a fast price adjustment via a change in nominal exchange rates. In this case the burden of adjustment lies only in relative price adjustments. Our analysis shows that distances in competitiveness have a negative effect on business cycle synchronization. The economic intuition is straightforward: countries with flexible prices move faster on the adjustment path to equilibrium whereas stickiness slows structural adjustments and preserves imbalances at the price of un(der) employment. Another way to increase competitiveness would be through gains in productivity, for example via the reduction of bureaucracy.

Figure 3 clearly shows that competitiveness distances decreased over time. For a currency union it is necessary for member countries to allow price adjustments that close competitiveness gaps. This includes, of course, unpopular measures that allow for nominal price cuts including wages. This way, real devaluations can happen even without changes in nominal exchange rates in due time and ensure business cycle synchronization.[2]

[2] Sometimes it is argued that expansionary monetary policy in countries with inflation rates below target might help as well. In case of a currency union lifting the target inflation above 2% is seen as a remedy. However, such policies only can potentially close gaps of competitiveness in case they affect regional inflation rates differently.

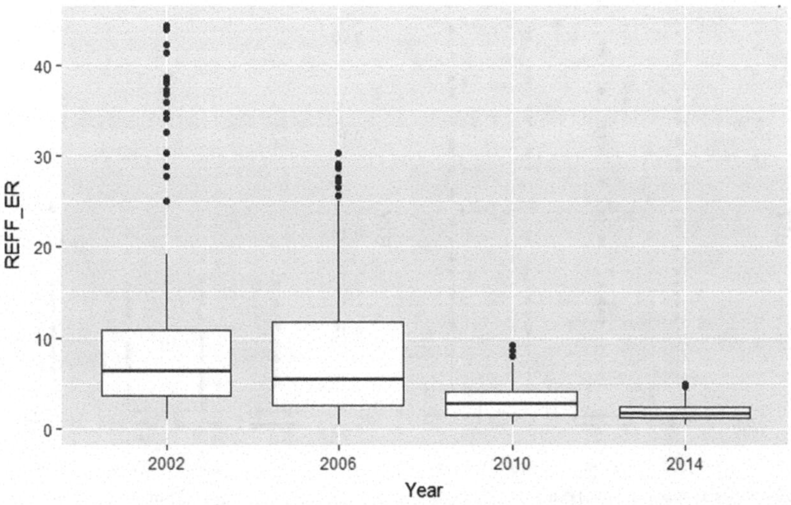

Fig. 3 Differences in real effective exchange rates in time (*Source* Authors)

2.4 *Trade*

Bilateral trade volumes are positively related with synchronization. Thus, policymakers should ask how trade intensity in the EA can be further increased without leading to more economic and trade specialization. This means that intra-industry trade that generally characterizes trade between industrialized countries should be strengthened. The EA members participate in the common internal market of the EU and do not have any currency risk. Although trade barriers are low, they still exist as nontariff measures, for example in national consumer laws, taxation, and prohibitive market entry requirements, especially on the market for services. Figure 4 shows relatively constant trade intensities or even declining ones in the last subperiod.

It can be expected that larger markets with their increasing economies of scale would increase cross-border trade within industries. Policymakers shall, thus, further standardize regulations across all member countries and complete the internal market for physical goods and services. This is especially important in digitalized economies which are characterized by high GDP shares of the service industry.

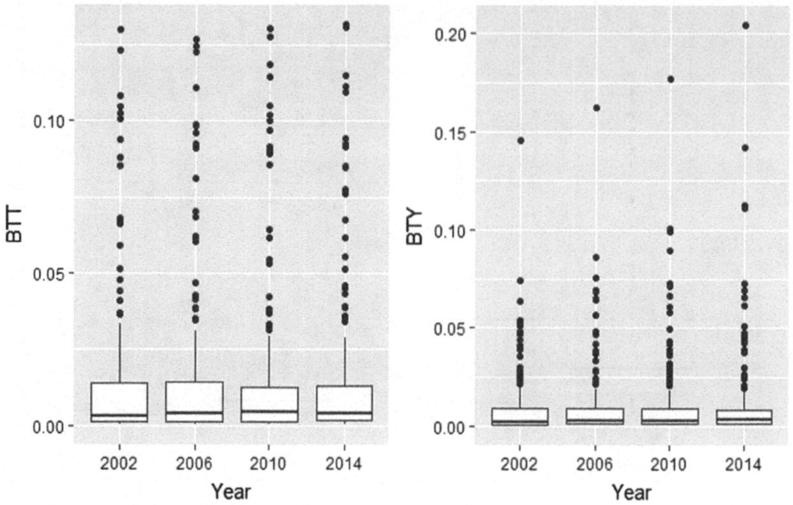

Fig. 4 Trade volumes over time (12a, l.h.s., in % of total trade; 12b, r.h.s., in % of GDP) (*Source* Authors)

2.5 *Other Variables*

It is important that bilateral trade volumes increase without further economic or trade specialization, which could play a role against synchronization. Policymakers shall, thus, aim to diversify the structure of their national economies.

Figure 5 (l.h.s.) shows that the typical distance in economic specialization has increased slightly since the start of the Euro and variation widened among members. Figure 5 (r.h.s.) shows no trend for trade specialization, but increased distance in the aftermath of the financial crisis.

Concerning volatility in nominal exchange rates, we can conclude that the Euro already solved this problem. Exchange rates are fixed with the common currency, which favors synchronization.

Summarizing, business cycles are highly synchronized in the EA in comparison to the benchmark United States. If, however, specialization increases, there is prospect of less synchronization in the future. Thus, it is important for policymakers in the EA to further foster bilateral intra-industry trade volumes and hinder distances in competitiveness. Differences in real interest rates and in fiscal deficits are already at low

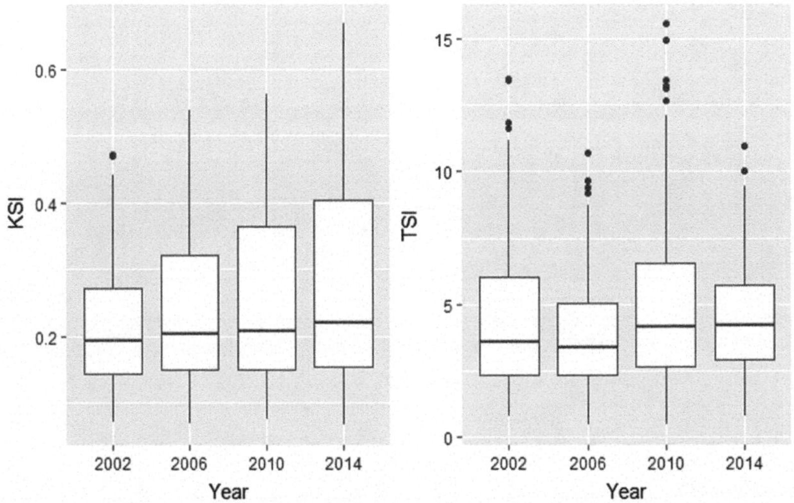

Fig. 5 Specialization over time (13a, l.h.s., economic specialization; 13b, r.h.s., trade specialization) (*Source* Authors)

levels. There is no economic agreement on whether policies should aim at further convergence in these variables because of side effects that preserve or generate new imbalances.

As a real uniform EA business cycle does not exist, there is a need for further stabilization processes which will be discussed in the subsequent two pivots. Like in the United States labor migration and capital flows might dampen the economic consequences from asymmetric shocks (pivot 2) and fiscal federalism might be the price to pay for having a common currency with its remaining imbalances (pivot 3). In other words, imperfect mobility that is even sometimes desired by local populations might require these populations to pay a price.

Reference

De Grauwe, P. (2018). *Economics of Monetary Union* (12th ed.). Oxford: Oxford University Press.

Appendix 1: Timeline of Major European Integration Events

Year	*Event*
1989	The Soviet Union disintegrates
1992	The Maastricht Treaty is signed, and the foundation of the EA is built. The convergence criteria to be fulfilled by member candidates are limits for the inflation rate, government debt as well as deficits, and spreads of long-term interest rates
1993	The Single European Market in the EU starts. The criteria of Copenhagen define the different rules to be fulfilled for those countries that want to join the Common Market. Among other rules, countries need to preserve the democratic system, respect human rights and follow a market-based economy[a]
1995	The Schengen Area (no border controls between the member states) starts. Today it consists of all EU and EFTA members except Ireland, Bulgaria, Croatia, Cyprus, and Romania
1995	Austria, Finland, and Sweden join the EU. They are former EFTA members
1997	The treaty of Amsterdam prepares the eastward enlargement of the EU
1999	Eleven countries introduce the Euro as book money. These are the so-called EA-12 except Greece
2001	Greece joins the EA, creating the EA-12
2002	The Euro is introduced as physical money and replaces 12 national currencies[b]
2004	The first stage of the Eastern Enlargement establishes the EU membership of 10 new member countries
2007	Bulgaria and Romania join the EU and Slovenia joins the EA
2008	Cyprus and Malta join the EA

J. Kabderian Dreyer and P. A. Schmid,
Optimal Currency Areas and the Euro, Volume I,
https://doi.org/10.1007/978-3-030-46515-5

Year	*Event*
2010	Creation of the EFSF (the European Financial Stability Facility) as a transitory mechanism to stabilize EA member countries that are under economic pressure. After July 2013 the EFSF does not get engaged in new projects
2011	Estonia joins the EA, creating the EA-17
2012	Creation of the ESM (European Stability Mechanism) as a permanent stabilization mechanism in the EA. It is the sole such mechanism since July 2013
2013	Croatia joins the EU, creating the EU-28
2014	Latvia joins the Euro, creating the EA-18
2015	Lithuania joins the Euro, creating the EA-19
2016	The UK votes to exit the EU, increasing uncertainty about the future of the EU and thus market volatility. The event is commonly referred to as Brexit
2020	The UK leaves the EU

[a]The Single European Market or the Common Market is the heart of the EU membership. Three non-EU countries participate through the European Economic Area (Iceland, Liechtenstein, and Norway) and one country (Switzerland) through bilateral arrangements. The pillars of the Single European Market are the four freedoms: free movement of goods, services, labor, and capital. Trade barriers—whether in the form of tariffs or not—do not exist. Furthermore, production factors are free to choose their location. In reality, however, there can be barriers in the form of transaction costs. Formally, transaction costs are "*cost of using the price system*" (Coase 1937, 390). Exchange rate uncertainty increases the costs for transaction on a common market. Risk-averse firms will hedge this risk, which produces costs. Thus, 19 countries decided to leave this obstacle to economic integration behind and share a common European currency

[b]The national banks of these countries still exist as independent central banks and are shareholders of the ECB. Together they form the Eurosystem, the actual monetary authority in the EA. The ECB Governing Council, which consists of the ECB's executive board and the national central banks' presidents, takes monetary decisions for the EA and decides upon monetary policy. The ECB and the national central banks execute these decisions and implement the common monetary policy. The Eurosystem generally is comparable to the Federal Reserve System (FED) in the United States which is governed by the federal reserve board (comparable to the ECB executive board) and consists of 12 regional federal reserve banks. Monetary decisions in the United States are taken by the Federal Open Market Committee consisting of the federal reserve board and the 12 regional presidents

Appendix 2: An Introduction to Multiple Regressions

The idea of this appendix is to introduce the reader to the method used for our estimations along the book. We selected a reduced model from Chapter 3 to give a step-by-step example of what was done and thus ease comprehension.

Thus, we start with a basic introduction on multiple regressions reflecting upon the existing types of relations between the different variables used in our models. We further deepen the discussion with reflections on the importance of the qualitative (dummy) variables used in our estimations. Additionally, we introduce the reader with the different inference tests used, including the overall significance F-test and the simple t-test to decide upon significance of regression coefficients. We further reflect upon the need of using the *AIC* goodness-of-fit criterion to analyze the quality of our regressions and compare it to the commonly used R^2 and adjusted R^2 measurements. We further discuss the challenges we faced in our estimations such as multicollinearity between independent variables and heteroscedasticity of residuals. Finally, we discuss some of the rules of thumb we used along the estimations to deal with these challenges.

J. Kabderian Dreyer and P. A. Schmid, *Optimal Currency Areas and the Euro, Volume I*, https://doi.org/10.1007/978-3-030-46515-5

Simple Regression and Robustness

We started each of our analysis (entire period, subperiod, and financial integration) by running simple regressions to explain synchronization with different single variables. We proxied synchronization through the correlation of cyclical components of GDP. The main idea of this initial step is to verify the direction of relationship of each single variable with synchronization so that afterwards we can check in the multiple regression models whether the signals of each respective coefficient changed. This allows us to test the robustness of our estimates in the final multiple models.

In order to keep our analysis short and to facilitate understanding, suppose we select the following variables to explain correlations: bilateral trade intensity (*BTT*), economic specialization (*KSI*), deficit differentials (*DEFDIFF*), trade specialization (*TSI*), and distance between countries (*DIST*). Table 10 in Chapter 3 provides estimates for the simple regressions of correlations on these variables, where intercepts are ignored. The simple regressions estimated are given by:

$$COR_{ij} = \beta_0 + \beta_1 BTT_{ij} + \varepsilon_{ij}$$

$$COR_{ij} = \beta_0 + \beta_1 KSI_{ij} + \varepsilon_{ij}$$

$$COR_{ij} = \beta_0 + \beta_1 DEFDIFF_{ij} + \varepsilon_{ij}$$

$$COR_{ij} = \beta_0 + \beta_1 TSI_{ij} + \varepsilon_{ij}$$

$$COR_{ij} = \beta_0 + \beta_1 DIST_{ij} + \varepsilon_{ij}$$

We can interpret the slope β_1 as the change in correlation for a 1 unit increase of the independent variable. Thus, if one looks at Table 10 in Chapter 3, we can say that when trade intensity, deficit differentials, economic specialization, trade specialization, and distances increase by one unit, the mean correlation is altered by 1.89474, −0.05947, −0.01347, −0.01409, and −0.00009, respectively.

However, it is important to check whether these parameters are statistically significant according to the student's t inference test with the following null and alternative hypothesis: $H_0{:}\beta_1 = 0$ and $H_a{:}\beta_1 \neq 0$. In case we can reject the null hypothesis, we can conclude that there is evidence in favor of a linear relationship between the variables. The student's t

statistic in this case, can be calculated by dividing the estimated coefficient by the standard error of the estimate according to $t = \frac{\widehat{\beta_1}}{\sigma_{\widehat{\beta_1}}}$. Notice that in order to be able to reject the null hypothesis, the value of t statistics calculated for our estimates need to be sufficiently high in absolute terms. Likewise, we could conclude the same when the probability value (p-value) above t is sufficiently low. Notice in Table 10 in Chapter 3, that the coefficients for trade intensity, deficit differentials, trade specialization, and distances are all significant, while economic specialization is not. The level of significance of 0.1, 1, 5, and 10% is marked in the table with the symbols "***", "**", "*" and ".", respectively.

Assumptions

In order to run the OLS regression method, it is important to assume different characteristics for the residuals, that need to be tested in order to make sure our regression results can be trusted.

1. When we calculate the mean of the residuals, we need to find zero.
2. The residual's variance σ^2 should be constant and equal to the standard error of the model. $\sum \left(COR_{ij} - \widehat{COR_{ij}} \right)^2 = \sum (\varepsilon_{ij})^2 = SSR$ and $\sqrt{\frac{\sum (\varepsilon_{ij})^2}{n-k-1}} = \sqrt{\frac{\text{SSR}}{n-k-1}} = \sigma$, where n is the number of observations and k the number of independent variables.
   Graphically speaking, residuals should present no patterns. If a pattern is identified when plotting residuals against the fitted values of the dependent variable and it cannot be corrected with the addition of other independent variables, we say that residuals are not stochastic and variances are, thus, not constant. This is evidence of heteroscedasticity, which can be detected using the so-called Breusch–Pagan test (BP test). Besides, as another possible pattern, a correlation between residuals could be identified, what would be evidence of residual autocorrelation. Here, the Durbin-Watson test could be used.
3. The probability distribution of the residuals should be approximately normal. Here, one can use formal normality tests such as, for example, the Jarque–Bera test. However, given the Central Limit Theorem, for a big sample size we can guarantee that the sampling distribution of residuals will be asymptotically normal, which makes the normality assumption less strict.

Residual Analysis

We can plot in our simple regressions the residuals against the fitted values of the dependent variables to check for heteroscedasticity. In Fig. 1 you find an example from the regression of correlations on economic specialization. Notice that most of the points form a cloud in Fig. 1, with a few points in the left corner. Thus, it would be a surprise to find a significant result in the BP test for heteroscedasticity.

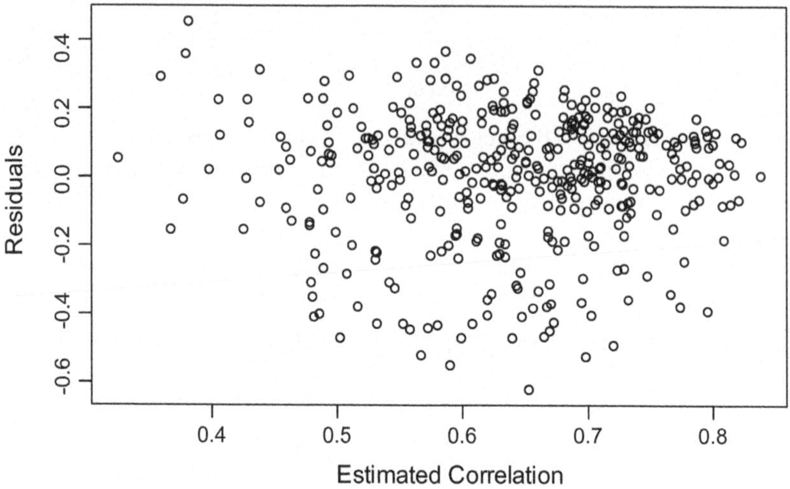

Fig. 1 Residual analysis (*Source* Authors)

Table 1 Heteroskedasticity and autocorrelation tests

Independent variable	*BP test*	*DW test*
KSI_{ij}		***
TSI_{ij}		***
$DEFDIFF_{ij}$		***
BTT_{ij}		***
$DIST_{ij}$	***	***

Source Authors' own calculations
*** indicate a highly significant, ** very significant, * significant and . weakly significant coefficients

Tests for heteroscedasticity and autocorrelation of our residuals of simple regressions of correlations on different variables are given by Table 1.

Notice that the presence of heteroscedasticity in residuals is detected in the case of the model with the independent variable distance. In all models, the presence of autocorrelation is detected. Thus, we decided to use in all our inference tests the so-called Heteroscedasticity Autocorrelation Consistent (HAC) covariance matrix (Newey and West 1987).[1]

Multiple Regressions

A multiple regression can be seen as an extension of the simple regression. The idea is that we add further variables in order to increase the quality of our estimations and reduce their residuals. Suppose we would run a regression with all variables we used in the prior estimations according to:

$$COR_{ij} = \beta_0 + \beta_1 KSI_{ij} + \beta_2 TSI_{ij} + \beta_3 DEFDIFF_{ij} + \beta_4 BTT_{ij} + \beta_5 DIST_{ij} + \varepsilon_{ij} \tag{1}$$

Ignoring the intercept, estimations results for Eq. 1 are given by Table 2.

Table 2 Multiple regression results on Eq. 1

Independent variable	*Slope*	*Significance level*
KSI_{ij}	−0.04724	
TSI_{ij}	0.09693	**
$DEFDIFF_{ij}$	0.09162	**
BTT_{ij}	−0.14789	
$DIST_{ij}$	−0.00008	***
R^2	0.235	
$adj.R^2$	0.225	
F-Test		***

Source Authors' own calculations

*** indicate a highly significant, ** very significant, * significant and . weakly significant coefficients

[1]Examples of HAC applications can be found in Dreyer (2012) and Dreyer et al. (2013, 2014).

The same interpretation for the coefficients that were done for the simple regression apply here, if considering all other variables fixed. Besides, we can say the same for the significance tests.

Quality of the Regression

The quality of the regression is measured by the value of R^2, which tells us how much of the variation in the dependent variable can be explained by the independent variable. How can we do this in our example? We want to explain with the different models the total variation in the correlations of GDP. Thus, the total sum of squares we would like to explain can be written as the sum of the squared differences between the observed correlations and their mean

$$SST = \sum \left(COR_{ij} - \overline{COR_{ij}}\right)^2$$

Residuals between the observed correlations and their predicted values according to our model are given by $\hat{\varepsilon}_{ij} = COR_{ij} - \left(\hat{\beta}_0 + \hat{\beta}_1 KSI_{ij} + \hat{\beta}_2 TSI_{ij} + \hat{\beta}_3 DEFDIFF_{ij} + \hat{\beta}_4 BTT_{ij} + \hat{\beta}_5 DIST_{ij}\right)$ or $\hat{\varepsilon}_{ij} = COR_{ij} - \widehat{COR}_{ij}$. So, the sum of the square of residuals we do not explain with the multiple regression model can be calculated as $SSR = \sum \left(COR_{ij} - \widehat{COR}_{ij}\right)^2$. Out of the total sum of squares one could also calculate the part that our model explains according to $SSE = \sum \left(\widehat{COR}_{ij} - \overline{COR}_{ij}\right)^2$. With this sum of squares in mind and in order to have a measurement of quality for our model, we can now compare the total sum of squares we explain against the total variation we would like to explain. By dividing the sums of squares we explain by the total sum of squares we arrive in the concept of R^2:

$$R^2 = \frac{SSE}{SST}$$

However, the problem of this concept is that R^2 will always increase when we add variables. As a consequence, a natural question could be when to add a variable or not. The adjusted R^2 offers a partial solution to this problem. If k is the number of variables of our model and n our sample size, the adjusted R^2 can be calculated according to:

$$R^2_{adjusted} = 1 + \left(R^2 - 1\right)\frac{n-1}{n-k-1}$$

One can notice in the equation that the more variables we use in a model, the higher k will be and, thus, the lower the adjusted R^2. Thus, adding variables that do not contribute significantly to the explanatory capacity of our model will increase slightly R^2, but on the other hand decrease the adjusted R^2.

Test for Overall Model Significance

Do we have enough evidence that our model explains a significant part of the total variation of our dependent variable, that is, that at least one of our independent variables is statistically significant? In order to answer this question, we can use the overall F-test, where the null and alternative hypothesis can be written as $H_0 : \beta_1 = \beta_2 = \beta_3 = \beta_4 = \beta_5 = 0$ and $H_a : \beta_k \neq 0$ for at least one k.

The equation for the F-test can be calculated according to:

$$F = \frac{\frac{SSE}{k}}{\frac{SSR}{n-k-1}},$$

where SSE is the sum of squares explained by the model and SSR is the sum of squared residuals and $SST = SSE + SSR$.

If we look at Table 2, we could say that there is evidence that at least one of our variables has a statistically significant effect on GDP correlations.

AIC Criterion

Developed by the Japanese statistician Hirotugu Akaike, the Akaike information criterion (AIC) is widely used in the selection of the "best" regression model. It is considered better than the adjusted R-squared for model selection and, *ceteris paribus*, aims at the simplest explanation of the dependent variable.

The AIC is related to the maximum likelihood estimation whose goal is to identify the regression parameters such that the data sample has the highest possible probability given that the variables are supposed to be governed by a random experiment whose parameters are unknown. Formally, the AIC is given by:

$$AIC = -2lnL\left(\hat{\beta}_0, \ldots, \hat{\beta}_k\right) + 2k$$

where L is the likelihood function giving the probability for the observed data. In the case of the multiple linear regression the first term is substituted by $n * \left(ln\frac{2\pi SSR}{n} + 1\right)$:

$$AIC = n * \left(ln\frac{2\pi SSR}{n} + 1\right) + 2k$$

The higher the sum of squared residuals (SSR) and the higher the number of independent variables (k), the higher the AIC. Consequently, models will be selected according to the lowest possible AIC.

Multicollinearity

The problem of multicollinearity is usually observed when we selected highly correlated independent variables (they bring the same information) in a single model. In this case, estimations will possibly deliver estimates that are still considered consistent, but with inflated variance, so that the methodology cannot be considered efficient any longer. There could be multiple consequences for this problem:

1. With inflated variances, important parameters are not considered significant any longer, given lower results to their respective t-statistics;
2. None of the t-tests can be rejected, when the overall significance test supports the model (F-test significant with t-tests insignificant);
3. Coefficients invert signs compared to what we would expect for their relationships with the dependent variable. This can also be checked by comparing the estimates of a multiple regression to the parameters estimated when running simple regressions with each independent variable. Note that the inversion of signs in the estimates could be a consequence of multicollinearity.

One can observe symptoms of multicollinearity in the results for our estimations in Table 2: the coefficients related to trade specialization and bilateral trade intensity changed signs compared to the simple regression models. Furthermore, coefficients seem to be generally less significant.

There are different ways to formally test for multicollinearity. A direct technique could be to calculate the person's correlation between two variables. The problem of the correlation measurement is that it only can detect bivariate collinearity. That is why in this pivot, we decided to use the so-called variance inflation factor (*VIF*).

One could use different rules of thumb to the level of *VIF* that indicates multicollinearity. Usually the value of 3 and 10 are proposed as cutoff points. In practice, it is well-known that *VIFs* higher than 2 can already predict problems in estimations results.

The most direct solution for multicollinearity is to identify the variable that causes the problem and then remove it from estimations. That was our approach in this pivot, when we constructed different "selection rules" to avoid multicollinearity problems.

Multicollinearity and Selection of Variables for Our Models

In our restricted example of the appendix, suppose we calculate the *VIF* values for the entire model estimated in Table 2. This would return the following results of the first column of Table 3, where the *VIFs* for variables trade specialization and deficit differentials are extremely high (*VIFs*> 100).

Table 3 VIF analysis

Model	*Model (3.1)*		*w/o* TSI_{ij}	
Variable	*Coefficient*	*VIF*	*Coefficient*	*VIF*
KSI_{ij}	−0.04725	1.01	−0.05229	1.01
TSI_{ij}	0.09693**	109.58		
$DEFDIFF_{ij}$	0.09162**	108.80	−0.00898***	1.03
BTT_{ij}	−0.14789	1.27	0.11037	1.24
$DIST_{ij}$	−0.00008***	1.24	−0.00008***	1.24
R^2	0.235		0.213	
$adj.R^2$	0.226		0.205	

Source Authors' own calculations
*** indicate a highly significant, ** very significant, * significant and . weakly significant coefficients

In column 2, we remove trade specialization and rerun the regression. Notice that both the inverted signals we detected before compared to the simple regressions disappeared. This shows us that the variable representing differentials in deficits cannot be used alongside trade specialization in the same model.

Using AIC to Select Models

As we understand that we cannot use directly the R^2 to compare the quality of different models, we go on with the selection of the variables according to the one that minimizes the *AIC* criterion. In this case, we estimate two models where we combine the five different variables to explain correlations in a way that deficit differentials are never used together with trade specialization. This leads us to estimate all possible combinations of variables of the following two equations:

$$COR_{ij} = \beta_0 + \beta_1 KSI_{ij} + \beta_2 TSI_{ij} + \beta_4 BTT_{ij} + \beta_5 DIST_{ij} + \varepsilon_{ij} \quad (2)$$

$$COR_{ij} = \beta_0 + \beta_1 KSI_{ij} + \beta_3 DEFDIFF_{ij} + \beta_4 BTT_{ij} + \beta_5 DIST_{ij} + \varepsilon_{ij} \quad (3)$$

The lowest possible *AICs* in estimations for both equations are observed when we use all 4 variables together ($AIC = -1336.9$ and $AIC = -1334.8$, respectively). Thus, both models are chosen with all 4 variables included.

Qualitative Variables and Regressions—Using Dummy Variables

You may need to use qualitative variables together with quantitative ones in the model. Imagine, for example, that business cycle synchronization depends on economic specialization, geographical distance and EA membership (EA_{ij}) to decide whether memberships make a difference. Here, the variable EA membership assumes the value one in case both countries analyzed are members of the EA along the entire period and zero otherwise.

$$COR_{ij} = \beta_0 + \beta_1 KSI_{ij} + \beta_2 DIST_{ij} + \beta_3 EA_{ij} + \varepsilon_{ij} \quad (4)$$

The estimation results for Eq. 4 are:

Table 4 Estimation results for Eq. 4

Independent variable	*Slope*	*Significance level*
KSI_{ij}	−0.02538	
$DIST_{ij}$	−0.00009	***
EA_{ij}	0.17336	***
R^2	0.267	
$adj.R^2$	0.262	

Source Authors' own calculations
*** indicate a highly significant, ** very significant, * significant and . weakly significant coefficients

This means that the average cyclical correlation coefficients for two countries is *ceteris paribus* higher by 0.17336 in case of two of the original eleven EA member countries than for country pairs that have not been EA members along the entire period. Thus, one interprets that EA membership increases business cycle correlation. This effect is statistically significant.

Note that in the main text, EA membership was defined in more detail. It not only could assume two values, but depended on the time ratio that both countries were members of the EA. Thus, this variable assumed values between zero and one. Actual dummy variables in the text are the three subperiods that measure the average in correlation distance of the three later subperiods in relation to the first four years of the Euro.

Interactions

Economic specialization is not significant in Table 4. One could imagine however, that EA membership interacts with economic specialization, meaning that the slope is different for the subset of the original eleven EA member countries. Thus, we could instead estimate the following equation:

$$COR_{ij} = \beta_0 + \beta_1 KSI_{ij} + \beta_2 DIST_{ij} + \beta_3 EA_{ij} + \beta_4 KSI_{ij} EA_{ij} + \varepsilon_{ij} \quad (5)$$

The estimation results for Eq. 5 are presented in Table 5:

Accounting for the interaction shows weak statistical significance for economic specialization for the case of the original eleven EA members. The negative sign of the interaction coefficient indicates that the positive effect of EA membership on GDP correlations is dampened by these countries' economic specialization.

Table 5 Estimation results for Eq. 5

Independent variable	*Slope*	*Significance level*
KSI_{ij}	−0.02249	
$DIST_{ij}$	−0.00009	***
EA_{ij}	0.21569	***
$KSI_{ij}EA_{ij}$	−0.20951	.
R^2	0.268	
$adj.R^2$	0.261	

Source Authors' own calculations
*** indicate a highly significant, ** very significant, * significant and . weakly significant coefficients

Subperiod Panel Regressions

In our subperiod analysis we used panel data, which means that we faced cross-sectional data for different time periods. In this case, different regression techniques exist including the pooling, fixed, and random effects models.

However, in this pivot, we use our models to explain bilateral correlations between different pairs of countries. Thus, it would be hard to imagine for example a fixed effect related to specific pairs of countries. Moreover, it would also be surprising to find an effect of the specific pair of country in the residuals of a random model. That is why we used pooling estimations for the subperiod models. In the coming pivots, we will revisit the discussion on regression estimations using panel data.

References

Arpaia, A., Kiss, A., Palvolgyi, B., & Turrini, A. (2016). Labour Mobility and Labour Market Adjustment in the EU. *IZA Journal of Migration, 5,* 21.

Artis, M. J. (2003). *Is There a European Business Cycle?* (CESIfo Working Paper, 1053).

Artis, M. J., & Zhang, W. (1997). International Business Cycles and the ERM: Is There a European Business Cycle? *International Journal of Finance Economics, 2,* 1–16.

Auerback, M. (2010). A "United States of Europe" or Full Exit from the Euro? *International Journal of Political Economy, 39*(4), 87–102.

Baxter, M., & King, R. G. (1999). Measuring Business Cycles: Approximate Band-Pass Filters for Economic Time Series. *Review of Economics and Statistics, 81*(4), 575–593.

Bayoumi, T., & Eichengreen, B. (1993). Shocking Aspects of European Monetary Unificaton. In F. Torres & F. Giavazzi (Eds.), *Adjustment and Growth in the European Monetary Union* (pp. 193–229). Cambridge: Cambridge University Press.

Bayoumi, T., & Eichengreen, B. (2017). *Aftershocks of Monetary Unification: Hysteresis with a Financial Twist* (IMF Working Paper, 17/55).

Berger, H., Dell'Ariccia, G., & Obstfeld, M. (2019). Revisiting the Economic Case for Fiscal Union in the Euro Area. *IMF Economic Review, 67,* 657–683.

Beyer, R. C. M., & Smets, F. (2015). Labour Market Adjustments and Migration in Europe and the United States: How Different? *Economic Policy, 30*(84), 643–682.

J. Kabderian Dreyer and P. A. Schmid, *Optimal Currency Areas and the Euro, Volume I,* https://doi.org/10.1007/978-3-030-46515-5

Bibow, J. (2013). The Euroland Crisis and Germany's Euro Trilemma. *International Review of Applied Economics, 27*(3), 360–385.

Blanchard, O. J., Eugenio Cerutti, E., & Summers, L. (2015). *Inflation and Activity: Two Explorations and Their Implications for Monetary Policy* (IMF Working Paper, 15/230).

Blanchard, O. J., & Katz, L. F. (1992). Regional Evolutions. *Brookings Papers on Economic Activity, 1*, 1–75.

Böwer, U., & Guillemineau, C. (2006). *Determinants of Business Cycle Synchronization Across Euro Area Countries* (ECB Working Paper, 587).

Cesa-Bianchi, A., Imbs, J., & Saleheen, J. (2016). *Finance and Synchronization* (CEPR Discussion Paper, 11037).

Coase, R. (1937). The Nature of the Firm. *Economica, 4*(16), 386–405.

Coe, D. T., & Helpman, E. (1995). International R&D Spillovers. *European Economic Review, 39*(5), 859–887.

Crum, B. (2013). Saving the Euro at the Cost of Democracy? *Journal of Common Market Studies, 51*(4), 614–630.

De Grauwe, P. (2018). *Economics of Monetary Union* (12th ed.). Oxford: Oxford University Press.

De Grauwe, P., & Ji, Y. (2017). The International Synchronisation of Business Cycles: The Role of Animal Spirits. *Open Economic Review, 28*, 383–412.

Dreyer, J. K. (2012). *Saving Based Asset Pricing Models: A Contribution to the Solution of the Equity Premium Puzzle*. Hamburg: Verlag Dr. Kovač.

Dreyer, J. K., & Schmid, P. A. (2015). Fiscal Federalism in Monetary Unions: Hypothetical Fiscal Transfers Within the Euro-Zone. *International Review of Applied Economics, 29*(4), 506–532.

Dreyer, J. K., & Schmid, P. A. (2017). Growth Effects of EU and EZ Memberships: Empirical Findings from the First 15 Years of the Euro. *Economic Modelling, 67*, 45–54.

Dreyer, J. K., Schneider, J., & Smith, W. T. (2013). Saving-Based Asset Pricing. *Journal of Banking and Finance, 37*(9), 3704–3715.

Dreyer, J. K., Wolffsen, P., & Mortensen, M. (2014). Wealth and Immigration in Denmark: An Analysis of Human Capital. *Journal of Academy of Business and Economics, 14*(2), 19–36.

Ductor, L., & Leiva-Leon, D. (2016). Dynamics of Global Business Cycle Interdependence. *Journal of International Economics, 102*, 110–127.

Eichengreen, B. (1990). One Money for Europe? *Lessons from the US Currency Union, Economic Policy, 5*(10), 117–187.

Feldstein, M. (1997). The Political Economy of the European Economic and Monetary Union: Political Sources of an Economic Liability. *Journal of Economic Perspectives, 11*(4), 23–42.

Ferguson, N., & Xu, X. (2018). Making Chimerica Great Again. *International Finance, 21*(3), 239–252.

Flassbeck, H., & Spiecker, F. (2011). The Euro—A Story of Misunderstanding. *Intereconomics, 46*(4), 180–187.

Frankel, J. A. (2010). The Estimated Trade Effects of the Euro: Why Are They Below Those from Historical Monetary Unions among Smaller Countries? In A. Alesina & F. Giavazzi (Eds.), *Europe and the Euro* (pp. 169–212). Chicago and London: University of Chicago Press.

Frankel, J. A., & Rose, A. K. (1998). The Endogeinity of the Optimum Currency Area Criteria. *The Economic Journal, 108*(449), 1009–1025.

Franks, J. R., Barkbu, B. B., Blavy, R., Oman, W., & Schoelermann, H. (2018). *Economic Convergence in the Euro Area: Coming Together or Drifting Apart?* (IMF Working Paper, 18/10).

Helpman, E., & Krugman, P. (1985). *Market Structure and Foreign Trade: Increasing Returns, Imperfect Competition, and the International Economy.* Cambridge: MIT Press.

Ingram, J. (1959). State and Regional Payments Mechanisms. *Quarterly Journal of Economics, 73*(4), 619–632.

Kalemli-Ozcan, S., Papaioannou, E., & Peydró, J. L. (2013). Financial Regulation, Financial Globalization, and the Synchronization of Economic Activity. *Journal of Finance, 68*(3), 1179–1228.

Kalemli-Ozcan, S., Sørensen, B., & Yosha, O. (2001). Economic Integration, Industrial Specialization, and the Asymmetry of Macroeconomic Fluctuations. *Journal of International Economics, 55*(1), 107–137.

Kenen, P. (1969). The Theory of Optimum Currency Areas: An Eclectic View. In R. Mundell & A. Swoboda (Eds.), *Monetary Problems of the International Economy.* Chicago: University of Chicago Press.

Kenen, P. (1995). *Economic and Monetary Union in Europe.* Cambridge: Cambridge University Press.

Koo, R. (2012, October 14). *Balance Sheet Recession as the Other Half of Macroeconomics.* Nomura Research Institute.

Krugman, P. (1991). *Geography and Trade.* Cambridge: MIT Press.

Krugman, P. (1993). Lessons of Massachusetts for EMU. In F. Torres & F. Giavazzi (Eds.), *Adjustment and Growth in the European Monetary Union* (pp. 241–266). Cambridge: Cambridge University Press.

Krugman, P., & Obstfeld, M. (2009). *International Economics: Theory and Policy (International Edition).* Boston: Pearson Addison-Wesely.

Lane, P. R. (2009). EMU and Financial Integration. In B. Mackowiak, F. Mongelli, G. Noblet, & F. Smets (Eds.), *The Euro at Ten—Lessons and Challenges* (pp. 82–115). Frankfurt am Main: European Central Bank.

Lane, P. R., & Milesi-Ferretti, G. M. (2008). The Drivers of Financial Globalization. *American Economic Review (Papers & Proceedings), 98*(2), 327–332.

Leamer, E. (1995). *The Heckscher-Ohlin Model in Theory and Practice*. Princeton Studies in International Finance, 77.
Lucas, R. E. (1976). Econometric Policy Evaluation: A Critique. *Carnegie-Rochester Conference Series on Public Policy, 1*, 19–46.
McDermott, M., & Scott, N. (2000). *Concordance in Business Cycles* (IMF Working Paper, 00/37).
McKinnon, R. (1963). Optimum Currency Areas. *American Economic Review, 53*(4), 717–725.
Mill, J. S. (2004). *Principles of Political Economy*. London: Prometheus Books and Pennsylvania State University.
Mongelli, F. P., Reinhold, E., & Papadopoulos, G. (2016). *What's So Special About Specialization in the Euro Area? Early Evidence of Changing Economic Structures* (ECB Occasional Paper Series, 168).
Mundell, R. (1961). A Theory of Optimum Currency Areas. *The American Economic Review, 51*(4), 657–665.
Mundell, R. (1963). Capital Mobility and Stabilization Policy Under Fixed and Flexible Exchange Rates. *The Canadian Journal of Economics and Political Science/Revue Canadienne D'Economique Et De Science Politique, 29*(4), 475–485.
Newey, W. K., & West, K. D. (1987). A Simple, Positive Semi-definite, Heteroskedasticity and Autocorrelation Consistent Covariance Matrix. *Econometrica, 55*, 703–708.
Obstfeld, M., & Peri, G. (1998). Regional Nonadjustment and Fiscal Policy. *Economic Policy, 26*, 205–259.
Oręziak, L. (2018). Fiscal Federalism and a Separate Budget for the Euro Area. *International Journal of Management and Economics, 54*(2), 85–98.
Overbeek, H. (2012). Sovereign Debt Crisis in Euroland: Root Causes and Implications for European Integration. *The International Spectator, 47*(1), 30–48.
Patelis, A. (2015). The Elephant in the Euro Room. In D. D. Thomakos, P. Monokroussos, & K. I. Nikolopoulos (Eds.), *A Financial Crisis Manual: Palgrave Macmillan Studies in Banking and Financial Institutions*. London: Palgrave Macmillan.
Persson, K. (2011). *Endogeneity and Specialization Theories of Optimal Currency Areas: A Comparative European Study* (Master thesis). Lund University.
Rose, A. K., Lockwood, B., & Quah, D. (2000). One Money, One Market: The Effect of Common Currencies on Trade. *Economic Policy, 15*(30), 7–45.
Stirböck, C., and Heinemann, F. (1999). *Capital Mobility Within EMU* (ZEW Discussion Papers, No. 99-19).
Storm, S., & Naastepad, C. W. M. (2015). NAIRU Economics and the Eurozone Crisis. *International Review of Applied Economics, 29*(6), 843–877.
Woitek, U. (1998). *A Note on the Baxter-King Filter* (Working Paper). Business School—Economics, University of Glasgow.

Internet Sources

De Grauwe, P., & Ji, Y. (2016). *Synchronisation in Business Cycles: An Endogenous Explanation*. Available at: https://voxeu.org/article/synchronisation-business-cycles Accessed February 3, 2020.

ECB. (2012, July 26). *Verbatim of the Remarks Made by Mario Draghi*. Speech by Mario Draghi, President of the European Central Bank at the Global Investment Conference in London. Available at: https://www.ecb.europa.eu/press/key/date/2012/html/sp120726.en.html. Accessed November 25, 2019.

ECB. (2019a). *The Definition of Price Stability*. Available at: https://www.ecb.europa.eu/mopo/strategy/pricestab/html/index.en.html. Accessed November 25, 2019.

ECB. (2019b). How Quantitative Easing Works. Available at: https://www.ecb.europa.eu/explainers/show-me/html/app_infographic.en.html. Accessed November 25, 2019.

European Commission. (2019). *Who Can Join and When?* Available at: https://ec.europa.eu/info/business-economy-euro/euro-area/enlargement-euro-area/who-can-join-and-when_en. Accessed November 26, 2019.

Friedman, M. (1997). *The Euro: Monetary Unity to Political Disunity*. Available at https://www.project-syndicate.org/commentary/the-euro--monetary-unity-to-political-disunity. Accessed November 26, 2019.

Friedman, M., & Mundell, R. (2001, May). *Debate on Common Currencies*. Available at: https://policyoptions.irpp.org/magazines/one-world-one-money/one-world-one-money/. Accessed February 23, 2020.

IfMHSG. (2019). Available at: https://ifmhsg.ch/2015/11/17/in-god-we-trust-all-others-must-bring-data/. Accessed November 27, 2019.

Index

J. Kabderian Dreyer and P. A. Schmid, *Optimal Currency Areas and the Euro, Volume I*, https://doi.org/10.1007/978-3-030-46515-5